THE BOOK
OF LEON

THE BOOK OF LEON

PHILOSOPHY OF A FOOL

by Leon Black

AS TOLD TO
JB SMOOVE AND IRIS BAHR

GALLERY BOOKS

New York   London   Toronto   Sydney   New Delhi

G

Gallery Books
An Imprint of Simon & Schuster, Inc.
1230 Avenue of the Americas
New York, NY 10020

First Gallery Books hardcover edition October 2017

GALLERY BOOKS and colophon are registered trademarks of Simon & Schuster, Inc.

For information about special discounts for bulk purchases, please contact Simon & Schuster Special Sales at 1-866-506-1949 or business@simonandschuster.com.

The Simon & Schuster Speakers Bureau can bring authors to your live event. For more information or to book an event, contact the Simon & Schuster Speakers Bureau at 1-866-248-3049 or visit our website at www.simonspeakers.com.

Interior design by Bryden Spevak

Manufactured in the United States of America

10 9 8 7 6 5 4 3

Library of Congress Cataloging-in-Publication Data is available.

ISBN 978-1-5011-8071-2
ISBN 978-1-5011-8072-9 (ebook)

DEDICATED TO

Mr. "Why Don't You Put All Your Bullshit in a Book!"
All Those Out There Doing Their Dizzle!
Those Who Said I Should . . . I Did, Muthafucka. Now What?!?
The Ruckus, whether you seek it or bring it!
All the Shit Talkers and Ass Tappers Everywhere!
(Matter of fact I think I like that last one the best!)

CONTENTS

COURTING, MARRIAGE, AND DIVORCE

RAISING KIDS

MANAGING MONEY

FUCK A FORWARD

𝕿hou hast madest thein divine judgement andeth procured my anthology of advisement of life loveth and death . . .

Change this goddamn font—give these people something easier to read, like Times New Roman, or better yet, Arial . . . And fuck that—I can't write a whole book like this! Damn, how did people communicate like that!?! I mean how would you order a slice of pizza? Or ask for your fourth refill of your Big Gulp? Don't get me wrong; contrary to popular, I'm worldly. Shit, I watch *Game of Thrones*. Like if I was applying for a job at Medieval Times I would pull this Shakespearean shit out my ass just to impress the interviewer. Have you ever been there? Medieval Times? That's that place where fine ass fair maidens serve you food while knights ride around on horses, which may sound nice but those damn horses shit while you're eating. I mean, the horses don't know any better, but they're fucking horses. What do you expect? By the way no disrespect to any of you people who work there; that's thou choice. Do you.

Now since I was brought up correctly, let me start by introducing myself. My name is Leon Black. Some of you may know me as the President of Hitting That Ass, while others may have heard of me because of my black belt in fucking! While I take pride in both of those achievements, I'm here to tell you there is way more to Leon Black than just my prowess in the bedroom (and living room, dining room, Laundromat, public library, ER . . . yeah I said "ER"—you'd be surprised). First and foremost, I am a Ruckus Bringer! I capitalized that shit because it's not just something I do on the side, it is my damn profession! You see, I am a natural-born shit talker! I'm a man who knows how to look life straight in the eye and figure it out! I'm a man who can take the worst that life has to offer and topsy-turvy that shit until I'm on top of life, choking that bitch out! The other day a friend of mine, one of those annoying types, always whining and shit—you know what I mean. I don't want to name names, but just to put a theoretical face to him, let's just say he's a white man with glasses and bald as fuck. Anyway, this annoying ass friend of mine was like, "Leon, you're so full of it, why don't you take all your bullshit and put it in a book!" And I was like, "Fuck you, Larry!" So I took that naysayer's words as a challenge (yes, I said "naysayer"—I told you I'm worldly) and wrote this damn book!

Now, from what I've been told, all books start with a forward, and since I'm not sure what the fuck a "forward" is, fuck a forward!

Now, this is a long ass book. I know: I wrote it. In it, I have done my best to share with you my guide to getting over on life. Not to mention the fact that a book has many other uses. Unless you're reading this on one of those damn electronic devices, you are holding an object that would make a good doorstop, an excellent coaster, and (if you bought the hardcover) an unexpected weapon. Think I'm joking? You know how many people are killed each year by dictionaries? That's where the expression "Words can kill" comes from. Why do you think they stopped those encyclope-dia salesmen from going door-to-door with those damn books? Because when people wouldn't buy them they would kill you with those damn leather-bound sets of books. Look it up. So look here, what I'm trying to tell you is that you can't put a price on the type of knowledge I'm about to drop on you. (Although Simon & Schuster did, and you paid it. I cashed the check—no refunds.)

So the way I see it, you have a few choices: First, you can either put this book down now, hide it away in a closet—or, if you're white, in a keepsake chest or a credenza and come back to it at another point in your life when you're ready for it. Second, you can wrap it up or, better yet, get one of those gift bags from the Dollar Store, drop the book in, and gift it (or re-gift it if it was given to you as a gift) to someone who is ready for what I'm about to lay down. Third, if you're reading this on a train, bus, or some other form of filthy public transportation, you can hand this book to the nosy ass person next to you who has been free-reading this shit over your shoulder since you opened it. Or last, you can search your soul and realize that you need this book, and you need me to straighten your crooked ass life out. If you choose this option, don't take it lightly. I'm not bullshitting you. I'm trying to help your ass, so before you have the audacity to turn down my valuable assistance, take a minute! Now, I'm sure you'll notice that there's nothing but a picture of me on the next page, but it's more than just a picture of me. That picture is a picture of me looking at you looking at me as you look at yourself. I want you to look into my eyes (please resist the urge to kiss me), and as you do, search your soul. When you're done and you're sure you're ready, take your damn dirty ass thumb, lick it, and turn the first page of the rest of your life.

THE BOOK
OF LEON

NO
TURNING
BACK

HE AIN'T WRONG . . .
HE JUST AIN'T RIGHT

Whoever you are and whatever your reasons, clearly you made the right damn decision to sit your ass down and read the most important book of your life! So, since you're here, let's begin.

You're about to read a whole lot of shit in this book, and trust me, this knowledge isn't for all of you, but I know for a fact that some of you will get what I'm talking about. "Who are those people?" you ask. If you have to ask, then it ain't you, because those people know who the fuck they are!!!

Now, people have different ideas on where and how to start a story. Some people like to start in the middle by saying some shit that sounds weird because you don't know what the fuck came before it. The problem with that is that if you don't know where the fuck you've been, you're gonna have a hard time figuring out where the hell you're going. Other, more creative people like to start shit toward the end, then jump to the beginning and then wrap back around to the end again. You know what I'm talking about? It's what they do in every movie about a singer. Movies about people like Ray Charles, James Brown, and—just so you don't think I only watch movies about black people—Johnny Cash. All of those movies always start with a dude looking tired and old as fuck. Like we're catching him a day and a half before he dies. He's always sitting somewhere reflecting on his life as he stares at something like a clock or a glass of water or some shit. All of a sudden everything goes black for a second, and then across the screen we see the name of some tiny ass town like "Broken Foot, Alabama," or "Chipped Tooth, Tennessee," and a date from years ago. At this point, we know we are in a flashback, so we are treated to bits of that man's tragic ass life, complete with all his fuck-ups. And then, like a flash, we see him old again. That's what we see, but the part that we don't get to see is that old ass man sitting there staring at a glass of water for two hours while people tap the fuck out of him to get him to snap out of it. That's a movie I would like to see: the day James Brown's concerned friends tapped the shit out of his shoulder for two damn hours. "James . . . James . . . James!"

Anyway, while I like that way of telling a story—I mean, they did that shit in *Pulp Fiction* too! I loved that movie! Samuel L. Jackson and John Travolta! Playing hit men! Who the fuck doesn't like *Pulp Fiction*? Besides I'm *not* trying to tell you my life's story. I mean, I will be telling you some shit from my life, but not tragic shit and not for entertainment's sake. I don't need you judging my life. What the fuck do I look like?! Huh? What I share is for you to learn from, not to mock!

Look, I'ma tell you right now, I know a little about everything but not a whole lot about anything, so get from this book what you need and don't complain to me about shit!

THE FRONT OF THIS DAMN BOOK

Did you see the cover of this damn book? Woo, some deep shit, huh? Well, obviously, that's me! Now, I could leave it there, but since this is a book and they're paying me by the word, let me try to explain the cover to you in as many words as possible. If I was to give the version of Leon on the cover a name it would be Ruckus-Damus. That name of course being based on Nostradamus, which sounds like it could have been a great name for a nasal spray. Any of you bastards with sinus problems or allergies know what I'm talking about.

Now if you are educated and know your shit, you've heard of Nostradamus. He was a smart white dude from years ago who used to make predictions about shit and for the most part he wound up being right. As a matter of fact, he has been so right about shit that some people think he was psychic. Now for those of you who don't think psychics are real, I'm here to tell you they are, because I damn sure am! And I'm not some bullshit long-term psychic. I mean, it was easy for Nostradamus to make predictions: He knew that he and all the muthafuckas who he predicted to would be dead by the time the moment came to prove his shit right or wrong. Nah, I'm an in-the-moment predictor: My shit plays out right away, so much so that I'm right there to say to you, "I knew you would fuck that shit up!" Not to mention, way back in 2007 I predicted big things for an unheralded candidate for president when I said I was Barack Obama and I was the president of hitting that ass. Now while I don't know what that man does in his private life, and I have too much respect for him to speculate (just in case you're reading my book, Mr. President—much respect!), he did become president of the United States, so as you see my prediction skills are impeccable.

That paragraph just earned me $54 . . . Cha-Ching!

BOOK CLUBS

lthough I'm telling you to read this book, I've got to be honest: I haven't read it. I'm just not a big reader. I don't have time to indulge in flipping pages. If I do read an occasional book, I do it while I'm watching the movie version of it just to make sure the two line up. Now, I don't mind having someone read the book to me—maybe a friend of mine, or maybe Leonard Nimoy on audiobook. That way I can multitask: I can make a sandwich, go grocery shopping, take a cooking class. You can't do any of that shit when you're just reading a book old school. You're wasting your life away like that, reading about what someone else is doing while you ain't do- ing shit. I'm too busy living life, making things happen, traveling, pleasing women. If your only outlet for social activity is a fucking book club, then you need to toss that book into the trash! Tell your book club buddies you all are gonna go out drinking, but instead, get your book club to grind up against some strangers. Live life, so that way YOU can write a book about it and get a book club together around your shit. I would pay to have a book club sit around in a circle and read this damn book! Have people talk about *your* life every week, analyze it, tell you how it changed their lives. Bring the muthafuckin' ruckus!

On a sidenote, my favorite books are the ones with the wizards. I love me some fucking wizards. The way they cast spells on people's asses and shit with them wands and their funny hats. How bad ass is that? Let me tell you something, if you see one of them damn wizards walking down the street, don't laugh at him. I'm here to tell you don't do it. One day you'll be walking your dog with your lady by your side and you'll see one of them wizards wearing that damn wizard hat and carrying that damn wizard wand and he'll catch you snickering at him, wave his wand and cast a spell on you and the next thing you know he turned you into a dog and your dog into you. Now you're a fucking dog man still wearing your man clothes and your dog is a naked you walking upright with your lady and all you'll be able to think is "You hatin' ass wizard, you ain't shit!"

But you can't say that shit out loud because he'll put another spell on you. Actually, you can't even talk because you're a fucking dog.

THE SHIT

Now, if you are an observant person, I'm sure you've noticed that I tend to use a lot of colorful words. Some people's curse words just kind of slip out by accident. They didn't mean to say them, they just got lost in the moment. People are so embarrassed when it happens that they cover their mouths and apologize. If it happens on TV, the censors bleep it. And if a kid does it, they wash their mouths out with soap. Oh yeah . . . let's just say when I was a kid I had the cleanest mouth on the block. That's because back then just as now I have no shame speaking my mind; dirty words don't slip out—I throw them out with accurate aim and purposeful intent! One curse word in particular you're gonna read a lot is "shit." If you've been paying attention, you know I've used it a lot already. To be honest, it's an important word that has many uses in everyday life. I mean, we all take shits every day—that's the base use of the word. But think about it: That same word that is used to represent the waste that comes out of our ass is also something we all strive to be. Don't believe me? I know, you're like, "Leon, what the fuck are you talking about?!" Well, calm the fuck down and let me elaborate! Say somebody came up to you, looked you in the eye, and said, "You ain't shit!" You would be ready to fight, right?

Why? Shouldn't you be like, "Thanks"? No! You would be ready to fight that muthafucka just to prove to his ass that you are indeed THE muthafuckin' shit!

Confusing? I know, but if you keep reading, everything will be clear. Because, trust me, this book is full of shit, lots of shit! So let this serve as a de facto disclaimer: I might say some shit that could come off as sexist and—if you're the sensitive type—maybe even damn near racist, but trust me, I'm not here to disrespect anyone. The shit I might say about you could easily apply right back to my black ass. It's just that today, I'm the one laying it down. What I'm saying is that if you just *hear* what I'm saying, it might sound messed up; but if you really *listen* to what the fuck I'm saying, you'll get the brilliance of it!

So don't write me no letters complaining. First of all, I don't open mail. You never know what the fuck is in a damn envelope, could be bills, anthrax . . . I don't know! And second, I don't have a legal address for you to send it to anyway! Look, if you're offended and wanna blame someone, don't blame me, blame the one who told me to take all my shit and put it in a book!

THE GOOD, THE BAD,
AND THE UGLY

*A*s I mentioned earlier, a certain party challenged me, and I am always ready for a challenge. Fuck around, lie around, don't come at me like that. Second of all, "bullshit"? You ever see actual bullshit? Bulls make big piles of shit, a whole lot of nasty ass shit! But then I got to thinking that I do have a whole big pile of shit to share with the world and some of it is nasty, so at the moment, I decided to write a manual on how to live life the Leon Black way. Now, you heard me right: I said "manual" and not "book." There's a big difference. A *book* is something you read, some romantic shit with long-haired sexy ass men and women making love on horseback. A *manual* is something you study, work with; it has diagrams and instructions. If you sit down to study a manual, it requires you to be ready to put in some hard work. Hell, think of anyone you ever met named Manual.

I bet that muthafucka worked hard for his money! Bottom line, you *write* a book but you *compile* a manual, and that's what the fuck I did! I compiled an instructional manual just for your ass!

Consider this book the blue shit swirling in your toilet. Sure, you could take that disgusting bathroom brush and clean all the shit out yourself. Or you could let the little blue hockey puck do the work for you. Lucky for you, I've been the fucking brush. I've been through a lot of shit, caused a lot of shit, flipped a lot of shit. I've been chased out of a lot of cities, counties, villages, museums, stores, strip clubs, bars, even a fucking pickle factory. Not anymore, though. Now I'm the blue puck. I topsy-turvied that shit. Now, people see my face and yell, "Oh shit! That's Leon!" "Leon helped me through a divorce!" "Leon helped me get laid!" "Leon helped me feel good about shipping my kids off to some expensive ass boarding school!" That's how I doozit.

The truth is, you *can* be fucked up and happy. I know, because as a fool, I've fucked up a lot. I've run my ass into the ground like a rental car. I've turned my fuck-ups into champagne-filled croissants. Not to mention, I can make my fuck-ups seem less fucked up than your fuck-ups. You see, the problem is that your fuck-ups have fucked you up. And all the advice in the world hasn't helped you stop fucking up. Because you've been getting the wrong kind of advice. You've been getting "good" advice. All that Zen-mindfulness self-help bullshit you've been reading: "Avoid carbs!" "Consume less dairy!" "Stay in the moment!" Fuck that.

Don't get me wrong, I'm not here to give you bad advice either. The last thing I want is you getting incarcerated. I'm here to give you good-bad advice.

What is "good-bad advice," you ask? It's the kind of advice you didn't know you needed. Answers to questions you didn't know to ask. It's the type of advice where the good just barely outweighs the bad— like when you buy your kid a PlayStation 4 for his graduation, then sneak it out of his room in the middle of the night, return it to Target for a refund, but tell him it was stolen by some white man. Of course some white man didn't steal it, but I'm just preparing him for the real world: stealing PlayStations, jobs, etc.—it's all the same thing. You know what I mean?

Well, I'm sure some of you did. See, your child got the joy of receiving a gift, learned a lesson about life and you got your money back—that's the Good, the Bad, and the Ugly.

LOW BLOW

The his book is about to come straight at you. It's like how in boxing, some fighters throw looping ass punches. Not me. I punch a muthafucka straight in the nuts with my shit, I don't care if I'm gonna get disqualified. See now my opponent will be so paranoid I'ma punch him in the nuts that he's gonna keep his guard, leaving his nose wide open for a punch that he'll see coming, but won't be able to stop it. That's the way I think, and I'm gonna give you shit like that, more outside-the-box ways of thinking, crazy shit you may never have thought of before. Don't get me wrong, I'm not going to tell you to do dumb shit. As a matter of fact, I'm not gonna tell you to do anything. I'm gonna give you things to consider. That way, you'll have a different way of thinking bouncing around in your head. And one thing I know for sure: You can't get arrested for your thoughts. Hell, I would be serving life if you could. Look, if I can just help you change the way you think in stressful situations, eventually you may change how you react. That's the way you change: You can't change all at once. You can't be Leon in an instant—only I can be me, 'cause that's how I doozit. As for you, you just have to look to change a little at a time. Don't go snatching that Joe Pepitone jersey off that stranger just yet. I mean, you may get that jersey, but on the other hand, you may just get your ass fucked up.

So brace yourself for some profound observations, practical advice, things I like to call "Leonisms." What are "Leonisms"? you ask. Leonisms are those little bits of clarity. They are bite-size morsels of knowledge that are easily digestible.

This book needs to be ingested like medicine. You can't just swallow it whole or you'll overdose from your own wisdom. You'll start living vicariously through me, wearing an open robe with a lost belt, house slippers, and a do-rag, and carrying a large plastic juice cup with "Leon" written on it. So I suggest taking in a chapter at a time; take a break after each, digest that shit, then jump right back in before you forget what the fuck you were reading.

One last thing . . . and before you say some shit like, "You keep saying you're gonna start the book, when is this damn book gonna get started!" Muthafucka, the moment you started reading the book, the damn book started—I did say fuck a forward!

EARLY LIFE

PEE-PEES AND
JOHNSONS

𝕴n case you don't know what a "pee-pee" or a "Johnson" is, they are both terms I'm using for your penis. I will also use the name "Dick." I know a lot of you white people, and folks in the porn industry use the word "cock," but I think "cocky" just sounds too serious. Shit, I prefer "schlong" over that—at least a "schlong" sounds like something fun, the life of the party!

Now that we got that straight, on to my point: For all you guys out there, you begin your life with a little pee-pee, you understand? Eventually you grow up and go through that awful shit called puberty. You grow that itchy ass puberty hair, gotta get your shots to keep you from getting shit. Some of you people even have to deal with pimples—all that shit is a pain in the ass. You can't wait to get out of that phase.

Eventually though, your little shriveled up pee-pee of a caterpillar turns into a beautiful butterfly of a Johnson . . . is what I would say if your Johnson was some soft, delicate shit BUT it's not, so don't you ever refer to your Johnson as a beautiful butterfly! At least not out loud—keep that shit in your head! Hell, for convenience I wish my last name was Johnson. See, a new Johnson has a certain kind of swagger to it! A good young Johnson will get the ladies talking—before you know it, your young Johnson has a rep. For clarification, a young Johnson can get a rep, but an old Johnson can get a rip. Oh yeah, you can fuck around and tear a tendon and wind up with a broke dick, take you out of circulation. So make sure to enjoy your healthy young Johnson. For years you have the opportunity to do amazing things with it and you had better, because, trust me, it does have a shelf life! Then before you know it, you're an old man and your Johnson turns back into a little pee-pee. You can't do shit about it, either.

Blue pills, you say? Contrary to belief ("Contrary to belief"—I always love that phrase, it makes you sound smart), that so-called blue pill is just going to give you an old hard pee-pee, not a young hard Johnson. Once you revert back to having a pee-pee it can never—you hear me: *never*—be a Johnson again. Which is good, 'cause your old ass body could never keep up with a new Johnson! It would fuck your back up! Your spleen! You would have blood going to all the wrong places! Fucking nose would start bleeding for no damn reason because the blood wouldn't know where to go! So sadly, one day, you'll just be sitting on your favorite recliner, lounging in your crusty old-man pajamas, sipping a can of Ensure, watching an episode of *Matlock* on TV Land you seen a thousand damn times, and your grandkid will walk in and yell, "Mommy! Grandpa's pee-pee is out again!"

A fuckin' pee-pee . . . Sad shit.

Now, I'm not here to guide all you young neurotic dudes who can't get it up 'cause you're in your head worried about stupid shit. My simple advice to you is calm down, stay focused, and make sure you're living in the real world. Nobody's fucking no famous actress or reality star here, so focus on what you are capable of. That sweet, sexy but borderline strange-looking lady in accounting, or the almost pretty waitress in that dirty diner who always flirts with you—potential successful scenarios like those should be your goal. Look, you're young, your Johnson is young, get out of your head and get out there, you have no excuse!

But you middle-aged dudes, your Johnson has aged with you. It won't be long before that Johnson's gonna go back to being a pee-pee. So take caution. Think of your Johnson like a car—you want to put some good miles on it. You want highway miles, not city miles, know what I'm talking about? For instance, you hook up with a fine ass lady and she takes you back to her place for a night of crazy lovemaking with her and her sexy ass roommate, that's highway miles on your Johnson. You can really open up your Johnson on a trip like that, see what it can do. Yeah, those are good ass highway miles! Now, on the other hand, you're at a bus station and you run into a not-so-attractive lady from your past and wind up hitting that in a custodian's supply closet, in between mops and cleaning fluids and shit, that's some city miles. You don't want to put too many miles like that on your Johnson. I mean sure, you're gonna drive in the city sometimes, but just know them city miles are fucking your shit up! With a real car, those are the type of miles you would put on a rental. You know, most people take care of their own car but they beat the fuck up on rentals. I wish there was some way you could rent a Johnson to run *all* your fuck errands— late-night rendezvous, cheating, escorts, you know, that kind of shit, so you don't fuck up your personal Johnson. And that way you don't give your lady no diseases, just drop that dick off and go back home.

WHO YOU?

Someone else gave you your name; you had no say in the matter. For all you muthafuckas with fucked-up old ass names like Herbert and Henrietta, I feel bad for you because someone did a number on your ass! Luckily, as we get older, making our own decisions and deciding who we want to be, we can give ourselves nicknames that represent us better. And yes, I know you can legally get your name changed, but that creates more problems than it's worth. You get that new name and start giving it out to people and they start calling you by that name but your older friends call you by the old name. Then one day you're at the mall with a new friend and an old friend is screaming your old name and your new friend is like, "Who is that muthafucka screaming at?!" And you act like you don't know because you're so committed to that new ass name and before you know it you're in so deep you forget who the fuck you are! It's not worth it! You can't tell your mother you're a new muthafucka! You can't tell your grandma that you're not Chester anymore! How you gonna look that sweet old lady in the face and tell her Chester is dead? See what I mean—some people go too far. That's why a nickname is a simple alternative.

Now, when it comes to selecting a name, really consider the image you want to broadcast. Mufasa is a powerful nickname. Let me tell you something, that name would look great on a license plate. You get seven characters to create your personal plate, so that name would fit right on there! And everybody loves that movie! Who doesn't get emotional when they think of the image of that fuckin' monkey Rafiki holding Simba, the newborn baby lion, up to the fucking sun! Powerful shit! What?! People will be behind your car, see that damn plate, and race up to see who's driving! That's why you gotta make sure that if you get a personalized plate, you pick something that represents you. Clever shit like A-Q-T is cool but you've got to back that shit up by actually being cute. And don't just pick shit because it fits. S-O-D-A-P-O-P has seven letters, but what the fuck does it mean . . . is exactly what I asked this dude when I caught up to his car. You would think he owned his own beverage company but that muthafucka just liked soda. Hell, I like soda my damn self, but worth the price of personalized plates? Nah I don't think so.

Or some nicknames just fit perfectly, like if your name is Andy, and you tell a lady they call you Andy-Conda. The anaconda is one of the biggest and most dangerous creatures in the world! Can you imagine that shit on a license plate? Do you know how many ladies would chase your car down to get a look at who's driving!?! That's called planting seeds! As awesome as Andyconda would be, though, you can't do it—nine letters, that's two too many. Drop two and it's Andycon, which either sounds like a criminal or a Comic Con–like convention filled with people dressed like Andys—Andy Griffith, Andy Dick, Andy Cohen, Andy Samberg, Andy Warhol, all the fucking Andys . . . either way you are not getting the ladies. Still, though, walk up to a lady and tell her they call you Andy-Conda, that's some different shit—that sets you up perfectly! First she's gonna smirk, 'cause she's gonna think you're fucking around. But you say that shit with a straight ass face. She'll probably ask you if that is the name on your driver's license. In that case, you look her in the eye and say, "No, but I can whip my shit out and show you some positive identification . . ."

Then walk the fuck away, just like before. Trust me: With ladies, you gotta plant the seeds any way you can.

For ladies, pick a name that makes you feel like you're on vacation—become a destination. Men love that kind of shit! Make sure it's a place that somebody would want to visit, though, something like Belize. See, that just sounds sexy and all-inclusive. Never—I repeat, *never*—pick some shit like Hackensack or Hoboken. No offense to anyone who lives there, but Hoboken just sounds like Ho-broken. Sounds like some place where your car would break down and someone would have to come and get your ass! Also, we all know wines and cocktails and exotic cars offer some of the best names (strippers have known that for years). But you might not know that some of your cute household pets have sexy names. Names like Bunny and Kitty seem like cute, harmless ass names, but go up to some guy and tell him your name is Katherine but people call you Kitty-cat . . . watch that dumb ass man melt, see, 'cause that's some sexy shit. And since I mentioned the name Bunny, I just want to throw out there, from my experience, Bunnys always have big asses and for some reason they all walk pigeon-toed. Don't know why, they all just do. Pigeon-toed, with them fucking knocking ass knees, with a fat ass, sexy ass shit. And not too bright, from my experience. (No disrespect.)

AND VICE VERSA

Let me tell you something: You're gonna learn early on that you can't fuck with everybody and everybody can't be fucked with—it goes both ways. So one of the most important things you're going to have to do in life is choose your friends wisely. You know how many muthafuckas consider me their friend but I don't consider them mine? I don't claim a lot of people; I'm a lone wolf. You don't need all that shit! Keep your circle as small as possible. And if you do add a new friend, remove a friend. Plus, if you have a lot of friends, you have to worry about your friend liking your friend. Nothing more irritating than going out with a friend who doesn't get along with another one of your friends. Look, I'm not gonna make this complicated. Bottom line: you need to find a friend who tolerates your shit and whose shit you tolerate—you call that a Vice Versa relationship. For example, you and your friend are at a club and you notice two ladies checking you out. Now, in the movies both of them ladies would be attractive, but this is real life and one is pretty while the other is ugly as fuck. A true sign of a Vice Versa relationship would be the two of you being able to accept the fact that one of you is going to get that ugly girl this time. Vice Versa is a way of keeping a running tally so that you never have to get stuck with that ugly girl two times in a row. Basically, your friend takes the bullet. He looks at you and says, "I got this one, brother . . . And Vice Versa, mutha-fucka!" And with that simple "And Vice Versa" you know you'll have to take the hit next time. Just know a Vice Versa can't be reversed, once the Vice takes the initiative to enact a Vice Versa. See, that's the number one way of keeping a good friendship: being willing to get the short end of the stick, knowing in turn you will eventually get the long end—Vice damn Versa! Now, on the other hand, if your so-called friend deserts you every time he gets the ugly girl, he is clearly not a Vice, he is a Versa. "Versa" from the root "versus," meaning he is against you. Once you identify that your friend is a Versa, I suggest you take your Vice ass and wait for the right mo-ment to Vice Versa him. This entails secretly switching up and Versa-ing him when he least expects it. For instance, in the situation with the ugly girl and the pretty girl, leaving him to deal with both ladies. When the ugly girl doesn't have anybody, she's always ready to go and drags the pretty girl with her. And as you leave with that cock-blocking ugly girlfriend telling her pretty friend, "Come on, let's go, Denise!" (I always found "Denise" to be the perfect "Let's go" name!), you get to look back at his shocked Versa ass and say, "redde est canis," which loosely translated from Latin means, "Payback's a bitch!" I know how to say that in twenty-seven different lan-guages. And Vice Versa, muthafuckas.

ROOMIES

Too many dudes live together as roommates. Whether they have no money, their parents won't let them live at home anymore, or their girlfriend kicked them out . . . there's no excuse! No apartment should have more than two or three sets of balls walking around, that's just how it is. Balls banging around sound like klackers (a dangerous ass toy they had when I was a kid—Google it) or, better yet, a clean pool break. If everyone lowers their TVs, puts down their cell phones, and shuts the fuck up for a minute, and all the guys started to walk around, all you would hear are balls clacking. By the way, the noisiest balls are long balls. Am I right, Larry?

Point is, if you're a dude, don't get a fucking dude for a roommate if you can help it. Think about it: It's a lot more pleasant to watch your roommate carry a bunch of clothes to the laundry and drop a pair of panties on the floor than a pair of shit-stained boxer briefs.

If you do manage to get a lovely lady for a roommate, try and hit that immediately. 'Cause if you don't, you'll be needlessly burdening your body by being fake. Men can't fucking pretend. I mean, shit, *Three's Company* ruined a lot of people's lives, spreading bullshit about functioning properly with two voluptuous feminine figures in your face all day.

Whatever your roommate situation is, be it shit-stained boxer or lacey panties, you need to take the term "roommates" seriously. That shit is deep. You are *mates*. Partners. Interconnected like fucking Legos. That shit is deeper than marriage—while you don't have no fucking contract, that bond is universally known and understood.

The term "roommate," I believe (Use "I believe" when you don't know for a fact, 'cause even if you are wrong, it's still what you believe) came from shipmate. See, if the ship springs a leak and water starts pouring in, you both go down with it. So if your roommate comes to you acting like you're his or her fucking therapist and says, "I just lost my job," you don't say, "Aw man, that sucks!" and give him a hug. You look him in the eye and say, "Hell no! You mean WE lost OUR job!" and "WE need to make sure YOU get another one so YOU can pay YOUR damn share of the rent!" Or if your roommate's crazy fucking girlfriend won't stop calling him, don't take him out for a night of vodka shots and Russian hookers to relax! You drive him over to a wacko's house, shove him onto the front doorstep, and say, "Straighten this shit out 'cause I don't need her psycho ass throwing a brick through OUR goddamn window."

STYLE MASTER

𝕴f you know anything about me, you know I have an individual sense of style. You see, I'm creative: I can take a little and stretch that shit. Now, I'm not the shopping type: I don't have the patience to go into some damn store and try to match a pair of trousers with some damn dress shirt—I've got more important shit to do. Plus if there's one thing I know it's that the people who make the clothes you wear have a plan! They'll make the collars on your shirts long as fuck and tell you that's what everyone is wearing, and then six months later they'll come out with some stingy ass little collars and tell you your long ass, hang-gliding collars are "out," leaving your ass stuck with a closet full of Goodwill shit and a camera full of "What the fuck was I wearing!" photos!

No, I don't shop, I *acquire*. A free t-shirt or a lost-and-found blazer here, a pair of sneakers hanging from a telephone wire there. Oh, hell yeah, I'll climb a telephone pole for a pair of Jordans, are you kidding me? I wish some dumb ass kid would throw more stuff up there, a fucking iPad, a book bag full of book bags—hell, if you're gonna throw away valuable shit like that, I'll be there to acquire it.

Now, as for, as they say in the white world, "acquisitions," you have to be open to what the market offers you. It ain't like shopping on Amazon; acquisitions come at you like great stock tips—you overhear it. You overhear someone at some fancy, seven-dollar coffee shop suggest you buy orange futures. Now, you don't know what the fuck an orange future is or what people do with them, but you got that tip and you buy it, and usually tips like that pay off. Well, fashion acquisitions work the same way: You're at a bodega (for the whitely impaired, think "specialty market," only a bodega's specialties are old bread, dirty sandwiches, and lottery tickets), and someone says, "Maaaaaan, there's some lady down the block throwing her old man's shit out the window!" See, now that's a tip that you better get on quickly if you really want to take advantage of it! So you go down the block and you scan the situation and you see drawers and t-shirts and run-of-the-mill shit, shit nobody wants. But then you see it, lying there by a hydrant, a poncho, a damn Clint Eastwood–looking ass poncho—now *that's* a valuable acquisition.

Why would a poncho catch my eye? you say. Because that shit is unique! That's the type of shit you make a fashion statement in! I mean, think of the damn term "Fashion Statement"! At the core is "statement," and statement means to say something! You're gonna tell me that if you walked into a bank trying to get a loan wearing that damn poncho, you're gonna tell me that's not making a statement?!?! Or showing up for a meeting with your kid's teacher, one of them meetings where the teacher is gonna tell you about your bad ass kid? You think that teacher isn't gonna think twice about saying some ridiculous shit about your kid!?! Especially if you squint your eyes at her ass like Clint Eastwood did in *The Good, the Bad, and the Ugly, For a Few Dollars More, Dirty Harry*, oh and I think he did a movie with a monkey, yeah *Every Which Way but Loose*, he squinted his ass in that movie, too. By the way, either the sunlight is always in that man's face or he needs some damn glasses.

But look here, don't get crazy with your statements. You don't ever want to get caught in a nightclub wearing pajamas. And you know the type of onesie pajamas I mean, the *Christmas Carol* shit with the dumb ass nightcap and the two-button trap door on the ass for lazy muthafuckas who don't want to take off their pajamas to take a shit. You show up looking like that thinking you're giving off a casual bedroom look, but instead you just look like you're a stupid ass sleepy muthafucka who should be home lying in bed drooling with a bunch of them cartoon ZZZZs coming out of your mouth, counting some dumb ass sheep. Which, by the way, I never understood why counting sheep was supposed to be some relaxing thing to make you go to sleep. Have you ever been around a sheep? They shit everywhere! They walk and shit, like elephants at the circus—they can't control it.

Why would you want some loose bowel ass animal jumping over your head while you're sleeping?

How is *that* relaxing?

SEX

BLACK BELT IN FUCKING

Just 'cause you tap a few asses doesn't mean you are an expert at tapping ass! Tapping ass is an art form, sort of like martial arts. And in order to become an expert, you must explore the fucking arts. If you are free of commitments, free of inhibitions, and free of worldly constraints, you owe it to yourself to tap as much ass as possible until you master the tapping arts.

And trust, just like martial arts, there are many different styles of fucking. Consider the infamous Shaolin Temple: Fighters would travel from near and far bringing with them their fighting skills. What they learned once they got there was that there were many different styles. As it is true with Kung Fu, it is also true with Kung Fuck. There are many styles; some people are experts at foreplay; some with positions; some master toys; others have extensive knowledge of oils, like baby and olive. I myself prefer coconut, but that's just me. To truly be an expert at fucking you must master all of these disciplines. So just as they do at the Shaolin Temple, the students are sent out into the world to hone their craft and in turn become Fuck Masters themselves, thus achieving the sacred and revered black belt in fucking.

Now obviously no one starts off with a black belt. There are many different colored belts, and each one represents a different level. There are a lot of different colors: The lowest level is white, that's for the person who hasn't even smelled a hint of ass. Once you see a lady naked (not nude, there is a difference), you have entered the game, and from then on you start moving up: touch a little nipple—blue; rub a little ass—yellow! You keep going from there: green, fuchsia, fucking taupe, the colors keep going, a lot of damn colors—just like there are a lot of sexual acts! Master a particular act, get a higher belt; the better the act, the higher the belt! Sitting at the top of all of those belts is, like, my name and the color of my ass: bee-lack!

Now, if you have a black belt in fucking, you should be able to walk into the bedroom wearing nothing more than that belt and tear shit up, no props or sex toys necessary. But you don't just get to be a black belt. I mean, you can touch yourself and others all you want, but to achieve true mastery, you need a sinsay. Now, what is "sinsay," you ask. It's like a "sensei" or "teacher" in martial arts, only in fucking it's called "sinsay" because he/she teaches you about sin.

To be honest, I think belts are such a good way to distinguish levels that we should use them in other places. Shit, wearing belts might help get rid of racism. See, if everyone wore colored belts, people would judge you by the color of your belt and not the color of your skin, that way they would be racist against your belt and not you. It wouldn't end racism, but it would be a start—because no matter what, you could always take that fucking belt off. It's not perfect but I'll keep working on it.

Or how about this: Companies should have belts instead of titles. Obviously, the boss should have the black because he's the one in charge, and then everyone should have belts below his. But, to keep sharp, the boss should give one custodian a special belt, one that's even higher than the boss's! It's like a personal belt, shit made out of suede or leather. That special belt should have no meaning to anyone but the boss. You see, everyone needs someone to keep them sharp, so that damn custodian should have the freedom to kick the boss in the ass every now and then.

As for martial arts itself, while I respect it, to be honest, when I'm walking down the street and I look through the window of a karate shop and I see a bunch of kids practicing karate with their parents on the side watching them as they strut around with their karate suits on and them damn belts . . . while I enjoy the fact that those damn kids are learning order and structure, I have to admit that, sometimes, I want to run in there and knock their teacher the fuck out, then point one hand over my head at 12 o'clock, and the other by my side at three . . . Just to show them kids what time it is. Then leave before the cops come.

By the way, if you never quite understood what bringin' the ruckus meant . . . *that's* what the fuck it is.

THE POHTA

POHTA stands for "President of Hitting That Ass," and I *am* the president of hitting that ass! You know how many asses in how many cities I had to hit to get into office? How many rest stops I campaigned in? You think it's easy to win Montana? No disrespect to Montana, but there is not a lot of quality ass in that motherfucking state *to* hit, that's just my opinion . . . I did say "No disrespect."

Don't believe it's a real title? I've included a letter below from the former POHTA acknowledging me:

It is with great sorrow and respect that I concede the presidency to Leon Black, who will be the next President of Hitting That Ass. We ran a great campaign, and I'd like to thank my staffers for introducing me to thousands of women who succumbed to my charms and made this such a close race. No matter how hard I tried, and how much I hit that ass, I could not compete with Leon Black's charm, skill set, drive, and ability to ignore all external stimuli/decorum and just hit that ass no matter the circumstances. I thought we had Delaware. I really did. The women there were challenging, but nevertheless, I plowed through with gusto. Despite my efforts, however, Leon proved invincible, and he not only hit the asses I already hit, he hit the asses of mothers, grandmothers, and great-great-grandmothers. He crossed lines I didn't know existed, and he did so with love, passion, and a real belief in the importance of hitting that ass.

I want to thank all my supporters for their tireless efforts. I still plan on remaining in the vibrant world of hitting that ass, despite not attaining its highest office. I wish Leon Black all the success and perks that the office of President of Hitting That Ass offers.

All The Best, Willie "Sweet Dick" Jenkins

See that shit! That shit is real! Respect the office, muthafucka!

VD GETS AROUND

With my rep of being the President of Hitting That Ass and having a black belt in fucking, I don't want you to get the idea that Leon is reckless.

Never, I repeat *never* tap some ass without protection! I get it, I've been there, I know how it is, nobody wants to stop the action, put their clothes on, drive to the store, to your local bodega, Walgreens, Target, wherever you go—I get it—that type of pause in the action fucks shit up! It's just like making some Oodles of Noodles, you boil some of them noodles, drop your flavor pack in, get your shit just right, then the phone rings. You don't want to pick it up, but you see it's your lady is on the other line, all emotional and shit, so you can't tell her you'll call her right back but you also can't eat them hot ass noodles while she's talking to you because you know you'll wind up slipping and giving yourself away and she'll be like, "Stop eating them fucking noodles! I hear you making them *hot hot* noises (those noises everyone makes when they eat the noodles while they're really too damn hot to consume), so instead you sit there watching them damn noodles dry out just like your lady would right in front of your face . . . so you see I know what I'm talking about.

Despite all that, I think some of you fellas out there take this shit too lightly. Part of the problem is because some of the terminology that is used, shit like *Unplanned Pregnancy* is misleading. See, a term like that will fuck you up because really if you have a miscue and wind up with a baby or an STD for that matter, you will find yourself in an *Unplanned Relationship*— with that lady, her husband, your doctor, and unless you are planning to be a deadbeat, your new damn kid! Do you know what it means to be a deadbeat? It means if you don't send that child support they will garner the fuck out of your damn check! Do you understand what kind of buzzkill that is? When you're expecting a check for $623.11 only to open that envelope and see a check for $206.17—buzzkill like a muthafucka! Oh yes unpaid child support claims will pop up anywhere at anytime, at the DMV, when you try to redeem a winning lottery ticket . . . trust just like that baby mamma you fucked and the little child you fucked over that unpaid child support will follow you for the rest of your life!

Now I know what some of you are saying, "Leon, every now and then the situation arises and I got to do what I got to do." No muthafucka, NO!!! Look, I know for some of you *tear that ass opportunities* don't come around that often! I get that shit! But that is no excuse! You have to look at those moments with a MacGuyver mentality! See, we know when MacGuyver is in a tough spot he improvises with shit so just imagine if all that stood between him and getting some ass was protection!?! You know that muthafucka would find a way! I don't care if all he had was an eraser, a shoestring and a chewed-up piece of bubble, you know that muthafucka would find a way to protect his shit while tearing some ass up! Hey MacGuyver, if you're reading this book just know, I'm a big fan!

That's what the fuck you got to do, use whatever the fuck is at your disposal but don't just use it, be resourceful with that muthafucka! Take something like a balloon, not a round one, one of those long skinny ones like the clowns use, they call them pencil balloons. Now you know you could stretch that onto your Johnson but don't just stop there, tell your lady to blow a little air in there and then make shit out of it, be creative. Make one of dachshund dogs or a fucking trombone, something fucking whimsical, ladies love themselves some whimsical shit! Know what I mean by "whimsical"? *Beauty and the Beast*, that's some whimsical shit right there.

Or suppose you brought your lady some flowers and she was so turned on by that shit that she wanted you to tear that ass up, but your dumb ass didn't bring any condoms? Well, you may not have brought condoms but you damn sure brought flowers and wrapped around them damn flowers is cellophane—perfect for wrapping your shit up. Now your dick is also a bouquet! See that, you gave her two bouquets! Sometimes the dumbest shit makes sense if you just think about it! Imagine how overwhelmed that lady would be if you handed her that bouquet, then opened up your pants and showed her that second bouquet! Ta-da!

Look, if the shit I mentioned earlier is too exotic, there's always the basics—Ziplocs.

Yes, I said it: Simple ass food storage Ziplocs keep stuff nice and fresh. Think about it, you could put a sandwich in a Ziploc and forget about that shit for days. Then one day you pull that Ziploc out of your pocket, open it up, and have that cheese, meat, and bread 'cause it will still be fresh. Fresh! And nothing like a fresh Johnson to keep a woman happy. Keep in mind this advice is for muthafuckas who are preparing to "Tear some ass up!" not "Make love." If you are looking to make love, you are probably in a committed long-term relationship, and I'm not tryin' to hate on your ass, I mean good for you but to be honest, this advice ain't for you. There are plenty of romance novels out there, plenty of them, I call them tear-jerkers; this book is not one of those. So out of respect for your lady and your situation you probably need to close the book now and put this shit down because this shit is for muthafuckas who tear up multiple asses . . . not committed muthafuckas!

MATTRE-ASSES

𝕴 don't think that people consider mattresses enough. A mattress is extremely important: You sleep on it, fuck on it, get sick on it and get well on it, you spend at least a third of your life on it. Hell, a mattress is way more important than a car, and yet I've never seen anyone get a mattress as a graduation gift. As for me, I've put a lot of thought into mattresses over the years and I've fucked on every style and size—twin, full, queen, eastern king, California king, Larry David's king, Wyoming king, and the extremely rare behemoth the 9×9 Alaskan king, orgy size—and I've come to the conclusion that I'm a Sealy Posturepedic man. I don't like that memory foam shit. You don't need a mattress that's gonna remember the butt print from the last lady you made love to. That's a recipe for disaster when a new butt makes a visit.

Plus, memory foam just takes, and trust me, you don't want a mattress that just takes and takes, you need a mattress that gives, one that takes a pounding and bounces back. Next time you walk into a mattress store, make sure you're prepared. Test every mattress. Throw a basketball on there and see how high it bounces. Throw your lady right afterward and see how high she flies. If she barely bounces, that's a low-quality mattress. If she bounces over your head, that shit is too much; you could wind up killing someone with an apparatus like that. But if you toss your lady and she bounces back up into your arms, you've found yourself a perfect damn mattress.

Oh, and mattress makers, don't tell me what the fuck to do—don't tell me not to tear the tag off. I'll rip that shit the fuck off if I want to! Also, I don't need one of those mattresses with the arrow signs that say "This Side Up." How do they fucking know what feels good to me or what I'm trying to accomplish? Say I just had sex with a lady and I don't want her staying the night, I'm gonna put the box spring on top of the mattress, flip that shit . . . so now we are sleeping uncomfortably on the motherfucking wood. She's not going to like that, and at some point in the middle of the night she'll roll over and I'll see the glow of her phone as she orders an Uber.

Problem solved.

THOSE TADDIES

This is a topic that is near and dear to me! I love me some damn breasts and the women who possess them! One thing I don't understand is men who are nailed down to one type of breast or ass. Look, as far as titties go, it's like this rhyme I heard:

Appreciate the titty you see today,
For they're all pretty in their own way.

That damn poem is as true today as it was when I heard it in the third grade. With that, I want to break down for you the three basic types of titties—four if you count fake ones, but I hate fake ones so much that I'm not giving them their own category. With fake ass titties there's a smell of plastic that makes me feel like I'm in some fucking sci-fi movie having sex with a way too perfect robot. See, I don't like perfection, I like a balance. If a lady has sexy lips, it works for me if she has a club foot. Or if a lady has perfect thighs, it doesn't work for me unless she has a sexy ass hump or something like that, see what I'm saying!

I was gonna do a section on ass, but basically there are only two types of asses, fat and flat, and I don't count the second one. Also, while big asses are desirable, just remember that as big asses get older, the one thing they don't get is smaller. Anyway, here's the three types of titties:

1. **The Bitty:** These are small to nonexistent. Most fat men have bigger ones than these. You might think they serve no purpose, but years ago I heard of a group called the Itty Bitty Titty Committee. Well, I went to one of those meetings, and lemme tell you, those damn ladies were some of the sexiest, most organized women I ever met. I wound up making monthly speeches at their meetings, where I discussed the concept that "More than a mouthful is a waste." They ate that shit up! To be honest with you, that was just some bullshit I had heard; truth is, if you had anything more than a mouthful, you would just put the rest of that shit in the fridge and have it later. Plus, who sits down to eat just a mouthful? I want a plate of damn food— a plate of food, seconds, and some damn dessert!

2. **The Titty:** These are what you want. These are what you marry! Big, but not too big! Goldilocks specials. They're big, but they age well. A little exercise and a supportive brassiere will keep a titty spry well into its eighties.

3. **The Tattle:** These are titties gone wild! If a titty is a container of milk from the supermarket, a tattle is a container of milk from Costco. It is a bulk titty! Most tattles are fake, but a rare special few are natural! Tattles can often be found in strip clubs and tend to demand attention. While tattles are great fun, they do come with a set of drawbacks. Often, big tattles are attached to big owners. Also, over the course of time, tattles endure a long ass journey: They see many things and go many places, and at the end of their journey there comes a time when they must lie down and rest, lay *waaay* down. Yes, the tale of a tattle is a long

one, there is no hiding it. Eventually tattles tattle on themselves, that's where the word "tattletale" comes from.

And lastly on titties, I'm not into breast reduction. If I was a surgeon, I would require three legitimate reasons to take the breasts down. You never hear of a man getting a Johnson reduction just because his jeans don't fit the way he wants them to. There are no dick reduction pills. Fact is, a woman has never said, "Oh, you're too much for me. Please take a pill to take it down." So the same shit should go for women, too!

By the way, one annoying thing I've noticed about the way titties are treated on TV by censors confuses the fuck out of me. They always pixelate the functional parts of our bodies. Like if a thong pops, they pixelate, or they don't want to show the part of the titty that produces milk. Censors got weird standards. In one hour, I saw the same chest in full view and then pixelated for no fucking reason. I was watching one of those extreme titty makeover shows, and it was about some guy getting a sex change. In the beginning, they showed the man's chest. The whole fucking thing, hair and nipples and all. The surgeons shaved him and then started drawing circles on his chest and shit where his new breasts were gonna be. They laid him on the gurney, put him under anesthesia, built him some breasts, and then cut to a month later when they took the bandages off. The music got all tense and shit. I couldn't wait to see what happened to this man's chest . . .

And *boom*, they took the bandages off and fucking pixelated the nipples. The same nipples we saw in full view twenty minutes ago, but now they're attached to a fun bag and we can't handle them? That's bullshit. They have no problem showing a fat guy with man titties, but a man with fake titties—that we can't handle??

FUCKABLE PROFESSIONS

ou can tell a lot about a potential sex partner by what she does for a living. I'm here to offer some guidelines so you don't fuck around with the wrong profession. Here are some random thoughts on the matter.

The first is a no-brainer: Stay away from Costco cashiers. Those ladies are used to seeing and handling large things. You are not going to impress them unless you're extremely well endowed. Stay in your lane . . . is what they will tell you, they tend to use a lot of shopping lingo.

Nurses are always a good fuck. They are caregivers and they know how to clean you up after sex—a nice hot towel to reinvigorate you, some warm coconut oil on you skin to open your pores, and an IV drip to replenish lost fluid. And in case of medical emergencies that occur during the act, having a nurse around just may save your damn life! As a matter of fact, for anyone over sixty-five, I say only fuck nurses, it's a no-brainer.

Now personally—and I can say this because I'm black—I like black nannies. You go to the park in the afternoon and you'll see a whole bunch of those fine ass ladies in all flavors. At really nice parks there's usually a whole selection to choose from. Why a black nanny, you ask? A few reasons. Black nannies know how to keep things secret. They watch their employers do all sorts of outlandish shit and they never say a word. Also, they are usually paid under the table, so keeping secrets is in their job description.

But the best part of being with a black nanny is that they'll treat you right. They'll fuck you and then make you a sandwich and cut the crusts off. They'll bring shit to your house in little Ziplocs (save them bags for later use), things like baby carrots, string cheese, healthy snacks to help you get through the day. These ladies love when you nap—they even tuck you in for your nappie-poo. They wipe your nose with the tissues they keep in their fucking bra. They are the best.

And you can be your true nasty ass self around them because they have a high tolerance for gross shit. You see, they spend all day cleaning up kids' snot. A kid's nose is like a caterpillar that blooms into a butterfly—snot is the caterpillar and the butterfly is the booger payoff. Children have so much fucking snot it's crazy. Where does all this snot come from? It's like a snotty ass assembly line. Kids don't have the sinus power to suck it back up like we adults do. No, on a nasty ass kid snot can't be stopped, and kids just let it flow.

On the other hand most adults have the ability to manage their snot flow. Like Viola Davis. What an amazing actress! She has remarkable control of her snot. If you ask me, I think she feels snot represents emotion, and when you let the snot flow it's like you're telling the world you don't give a shit what they think . . . give me my fucking Oscar!

4 PLAY

$\mathfrak{I}$f you ask me, foreplay is for someone who lost his pinkie or his thumb, because if you have five fucking fingers you should be practicing, "fiveplay." What I'm saying is, don't hold anything back when it comes to foreplay!

Also, one misconception is that foreplay happens right before sex. HELL NO! Foreplay is not what you do the moment you get in bed—foreplay is the shit you do all day long that gets your woman aroused and into bed. And trust me, foreplay does not have to be dirty or obscene. Don't get me wrong, sending your lady a text in the middle of the day that says, "I'm gonna wear your pussy out tonight!" will probably work, but so will sending a text that says, "Usually we spoon, but tonight we're gonna fork!" could work too!

And foreplay doesn't have to be expensive either. Obviously, you could take your lady to a fancy restaurant and spend a whole lot of money—I'm sure that would get you some dinner ass—but trust me, there's a better way. I have a move that I call the "Birthday Trick." Take your lady to one of those chain restaurants, like a Chili's or a Red Lobster or a Cheesecake Factory, and secretly tell your waiter that it's your lady's birthday. See, places like that make a big deal over birthdays. They make their whole damn staff gather 'round and sing a birthday song. You'll notice I said "birthday song" and not "Happy Birthday" because they don't sing the traditional "Happy Birthday"—they create their own shit complete with clapping and stomping and whatnot. To be honest, it's kind of fucking crazy; you wind up sitting there wondering why they don't just sing the regular song or at least the Stevie Wonder version. I mean, what? They couldn't get the rights? Is it a pride thing?

Anyway, you'll be sitting there with your lady, and all of a sudden they'll come over chanting and stomping, carrying a piece of cake with a sparkler sticking out that looks like one of those cartoon sticks of dynamite in it. It's a fucking spectacle, like when someone orders Bottle Service in the VIP section at a hot club. As that mob approaches and your lady realizes that they are coming for her, she will begin to try and tell them it's not her birthday. At which point, put two fingers on her lips and give her a "Shhhh." That simple, cool act by you will put a sly smile on her face. And as you share that free piece of cake ('cause those places give you gigantic pieces of cake for free on birthdays), the two of you lovers will enjoy a secret glance, knowing that you are getting over on the man.

Later on that night, call her "the birthday girl" and ask to see her "birthday suit." She'll giggle and say something like, "You know it's not my birthday." To which you reply, "Every day is your birthday." Right there, it's a wrap—you might have to splint your Johnson to handle the evening you have ahead of you! And as if getting some great sex out of the deal isn't enough, that birthday covers you the next time you forget her actual birthday.

The Birthday Trick—dang, that was some insightful shit! Hell, I think I'm giving you bookworms a little too much help! Anyway, happy birthday, muthafuckas!

CALL OF THE WILD

I know this might sound strange, but if you ask me, a giraffe is one of the sexiest animals on earth. Think about it: them long ass muscular legs . . . like the ones you see when you're on vacation in the Caribbean. When you go to one of them islands there are always some performers up on some stilts wearing masks, dancing around and shit! I would love to be one of those guys! You got to watch your lady around them muthafuckas though. Ladies on vacation get wild and you'll wind up losing track of your lady and come to find out one of them Caribbean stilt muthafuckas took her back to your room and broke her the fuck off. Oh she will deny it, but the evidence will be clear when you go up to your room and see hand prints all over the damn ceiling. Could've taken them damn stilts . . . freaky stilt dancing muthafucka!

Anyway, I would get me some stilts and a giraffe outfit and go fuck me a giraffe because goddammit, it's a beautiful creature. I love a good giraffe. What!?! Those flirty ass long eyelashes! I would tear that giraffe's ass up! They gotta use more of them in fashion shows, 'cause they can walk up and down that runway and wear more than one pair of pants at a time. I would like to see a giraffe in some heels, some sexy stilettos, with a garter that goes up to her thigh, or some fishnet stockings, that would change the whole game!

Ironically, I would fuck a giraffe doggy style, which brings me to this: Why do they call it "doggie style"? No animals do it in the missionary position, they *all* do it doggie style! So why not call it "moose style"? Why not "giraffe style"? Why is it "doggie style" no matter who the fuck is doing it! Oh, and especially cats, cats hate dogs and they gotta do it "doggie style"! That don't make any damn sense! Look, cats go buck wild, they fuck in alleys, dumpsters, even when cats are fighting they sound like they're fucking! Cats are so noisy and wild you never know what they're doing, they could be doing reverse cowgirl style for all we know. Sound ridiculous? Possibly.

By the way, the editor has informed me that fucking a giraffe is illegal, so just forget I said all that shit. As a matter of fact, tear this page out and throw it away. I'm not trying to go to jail for fucking a giraffe, especially when it was consensual.

COURTING, MARRIAGE, AND DIVORCE

SIGN LANGUAGE

oroscopes can be useful for a lot of things. Not everything, though. I mean, they're not gonna tell you if you're gonna get fired, or if you're gonna buy a new recliner. But they are helpful as a guide to who you might be compatible with. And in the end, that's all we really care about: who we're gonna fuck, or marry, or have kids with. Am I right?

SAGITTARIUS: I'm starting here 'cause this is my sign. I'm half-horse, half-man, with a fucking bow and arrow in my hand. I got three things going on! I'm a grown fucking man with a mane of fucking hair and a powerful chest, and I got horse legs and a horse ass, and a horse torso on my fucking body. With all of that going for me, I have to be wise who I match myself up with.

PISCES: I would get along with a Pisces because I like fish, and there are two of them. Would I fry them? Or bake or broil? Either way, I fucking love fish. I'll put my bow and arrow down and stand at the table and eat that fish. I'll stand, 'cause it's impossible to sit down with a horse ass.

GEMINI: Ahh . . . The Twins. What man wouldn't want to get with two fucking twins? These are two beautiful ass women. I would take them and they would be perfect for me. 'Cause it's no secret: A dude with a horse body is hung like a fucking horse! Those zodiac people knew what they were doing, 'cause they could have easily reversed it and given us a horse upper body and a man's ass. Either way, it's fucking confusing: Do I have four legs or two legs? Do I wear two pairs of pants, or one pair along with some shoes and a shirt? I don't fucking know. Is there a urinal designed for a half-horse, half-man body? There should be. And they should use Sagittarians for horse races. Get rid of jockeys. Tiny ass useless muthafuckas. Just imagine, if I won, I would walk my half-horse ass over to my bookie and pick up my damn money. I would have that winner's ribbon around my neck and I would be in the winner's circle, tapping my hooves and counting my fucking money. I would post the fuck out of that on Instagram!

LEO: Ahhh . . . Leo the Lion. A Leo is king of the jungle, but that's about it. Everything else is not his jurisdiction. He can't do shit in the city or on concrete. The only lions you see in the city are in a fucking cage at the zoo. Of course, there are women who are Leos, but the weird thing is that Leo, with that big 1970s-looking mane, is clearly a male lion, not a lioness. So does that mean that chick Leos have male tendencies? That shit doesn't sound right. I say stay away.

LIBRA: I like that the lady is blindfolded and holding a scale. It means she's judging the weight of our relationship, but she's willing to let things slide, so me and Libra would definitely get along. Plus, sexually, I'm into blindfolds.

AQUARIUS: Look at this asshole, pouring water out of a big ass goddamn beaker. We won't get along. All Aquarians are bed wetters. The last thing I want to do is be in a relationship with a fucking bed wetter. Golden showers are not my thing.

SCORPIO: A scorpion is a dangerous fucking animal. Why would they use it as a sign anyway? You don't want to date a Scorpio, 'cause they have the ability to poison your ass. They bite you, then you gotta get to the hospital to get someone to suck that venom out before you die. Shit like that would create a whole new set of problems for me. I mean, as a Sagittarius, what do I do? Do I rush myself to a veterinarian or go to the ER and tell them I'm a man who brought a horse in for treatment?

CANCER: Why that name? I mean, it's unfortunate enough to be named after such a horrible disease, but then you've got another damn affliction as your symbol. I feel bad for these muthafuckas. As if cancer wasn't bad enough, you also got crabs. Woo, I hate me some crabs! Nothing worse than crabs in your pubic hair. That's why crabs are always in a bad mood, living in some damn pubic hair. I'ma be honest with you, I've had crabs, several times. You could even call me a regular at the clinic. I'll pop into the doctor's office and she'll say, "Oh, you again," all snide and shit. I always wanna tell her, "Why don't you just shampoo my pubic hair and shut the fuck up!" But you don't want to mess with a doctor in her own environment. Never know: Catch her on a bad day, she might just cut you up with a goddamn scalpel, stick it in your ass like a shank.

TAURUS: The Bull. I'd like to see a Taurus fuck an Aries. How cool would that be? A bull fucking a ram. I wanna be a matchmaker on this one. The question is, who would wind up fucking who? Would the ram fuck the bull, or vice versa? Put them both in the same cell block to see who the fuck comes out. One of them will get fucked. I'd watch that episode of *Orange Is the New Black* in a heartbeat.

CAPRICORN: Half-fish, half-goat. That might be the worst fucking sign there ever was. Goatfish. Sounds like a dish you get at a Jamaican restaurant. You get to the ER with food poisoning and tell them you ate some goatfish, they'll just tell you, "You're an idiot for eating that shit. You deserve it." And are you telling me I gotta lay in bed, with my half-man, half-horse body, and try and get romantic with a fucking goatfish? We would be like two fucking idiots in that goddamn bed. My horse dick thwacking around, while she's dragging her fin across my face. That shit would start bad and end badly. I'm picturing her kicking me in the horse balls with her powerful ass goat legs. I'm not into some ball torture!

VIRGO: Virgo's a weird one. She's a virgin, and who the fuck wouldn't want to have sex with a virgin?! Then again, if she's a thirty-five-year-old virgin, shit can get a little hairy, literally. It's like if you put something in storage, when you open it five or six years later, you gotta know there's a good possibility it could very well be wrinkled and moldy. So if you're contemplating fucking a thirty-five-year-old virgin, take into consideration how long her shit's been in storage.

ARIES: Now I know I talked earlier about Aries the Ram fucking around with Taurus the Bull, but now I want to talk about it fucking with me. See this one is tough. Now remember,

I'm a Sagittarius, part horse with a strong ass horse body. Here comes a damn Aries Ram. A Ram is a powerful-looking animal with round muscular hindquarters—sexy! Problem is it still has a Ram head and Rams have long ass faces. A Ram lady is like an unattractive athlete, sexy while she's competing but not so sexy at the post-game press conference. Plus Rams like to butt heads, that means they like to argue, and the last thing you need when you come home late one night is some long-face Ram screaming at you, talking about, "Where you been?!" right before she bucks you unconscious.

MOUTH ON YOU

Certain shit makes me excited, like a woman with a smart ass mouth. I love that you don't know what's going to upset them, what they're gonna say or do when they get up, and best of all, how intense that makeup sex will be. Take it from me, a relationship should not always be blissful; that's boring ass shit. Too many muthafuckas want serenity, but you need bumps in the road, they give you character. Now, when I say "bumps," I don't mean potholes or craters, but more like when a woman gets so pissed she'll leave your shit out on the sidewalk, like everything you own—all your underwear, your papers, your reclining chair—that's a damn bump!

And you always need to treat your relationship like you would treat your job: Leave only one cardboard box full of stuff at her house. The last thing you want when you get fired from your job is to have to make two or three trips, and the last thing you want when you break up is to leave that crazy lady with a lot of your stuff. As much as I love a smart-mouth woman, one of the many dangers of being with one is that at any moment she could get mad at you and destroy all of your belongings. And trust me, she will get creative with her destruction. If you're lucky, the more easygoing ones tend to leave your shit out on the street. Some of your angrier ones tend to light your shit on fire, while other really cruel ones bleach your shit. I know fire sounds like the bad one, but bleach is hard fucking core. To be honest, I'd rather they burn my shit than bleach it. See, if your shit is burned, it's done, no question about it; but with bleached stuff you will inevitably make the mistake of trying to salvage things. Truth is, you've got to let your bleached shit go—I mean, you'll never be able to tell your red shirt from your white shirt because you'll be stuck with a pile of pink shirts.

I can't stress enough how bad bleach is—or, more precisely, how bad "Murder Bleach" is. On TV the only thing they use bleach for is to clean up a murder. Now, not every bleach is Murder Bleach. Brand-name bleaches like Clorox, that's for clothing, to take spaghetti sauce stains from a white tank top and shit like that. Clorox can't be used for cleaning murders 'cause then they'd be advocating murder and they would make the crime scene smell like a summer breeze or a tropical forest. Murder Bleach is the bleach that comes in a big ass white container and says "Bleach" on it—no damn brand name, just "Bleach" . . . that's Murder Bleach.

COURTIN'

$\mathfrak{F}$uck the financial burden of traditional courtship: dating, flowers, a shitload of pointless restaurants. The most important part of courtship is making sure your stuff and her stuff line up. When I say "stuff," I mean *your* Johnson and *her* vagina.

How you go about lining your stuff up is important. Don't try checking it while you're in bed lying down, that's too easy. You gotta stand facing each other 'cause you may want to make love standing up sometimes, like in a closet or—if you're white—on an airplane to join what they call "the mile-high club." Black people can't get away with shit like that. A white couple comes out of an airline bathroom all disheveled and shit, the flight attendant will just smirk and give a naughty *tsk-tsk* with her fingers to the couple. Have a black couple fall out of that bathroom, what do you think would happen!?! In a few words, Taser and YouTube video! It's just as well—black folk have way too much ass to fuck in one of them tiny ass bathrooms!

Back to lining up; once you check alignment, time to take a test drive. Understand this: Alignment isn't just about height, it's about how you fit together in many different ways. Make sure her skin doesn't make your skin itchy, like this one lady who had some weird contagious eczema shit. Her shit was so bad she could light a match off her ass like those cartoon characters do. It was some wild shit to see up close. Make sure you own a onesie pajama with a button-up latch in your private area for relieving yourself and for all sexual situations where you don't want to make skin-to-skin contact.

If you don't have a onesie and you want to have sex with someone whose skin is sketchy, there's always olive oil. Olive oil is a magical lubricant for face and body. If you rub your whole body with it, what you're doing is creating a protective coating to keep your skin safe from whatever the fuck they have. But none of that extra virgin bullshit! What the fuck is that about? How could it be *extra* virgin? Extra virgin? Sure, that's every man's dream, but that's just some greedy shit. As if plain virgin ain't good enough. Dammit, you'll never be satisfied! And let me tell you something, when you think about it, you don't really want an extra virgin. You will break your dick trying to get into that shit. And if you do get in there, you probably won't be able to get out. You wanna end up in the ER lying on a gurney with your dick inside this extra virgin Catholic chick, the hospital so embarrassed that they have to cover the two of you with a sheet? And next thing you know, her fucking religious ass parents show up looking disappointed in her and disgusted at you!?!

Lastly, when courting, always keep your shit well groomed. This goes for both genders. Always make a point of keeping a clean-shaven face: That way you don't cause any skin irritations on your lover—except if she's into the whole hipster beard with that curly handlebar moustache shit. And if you want to get into some kinky shit, clean each other like monkeys do—that's primal shit. Now, I'm not telling you to pick lice off someone's head and eat them, I mean serious, deep cleaning.

Sit your ass in one of those big ass round metal tubs, then grab some cleaning instruments and start scrubbing. I'm talking using Q-tips and toothbrushes, making sure to get into every nook and cranny on each other's body. Going places where the sun don't shine. That's real courtin' right there.

TATS

Look, I'm not gonna tell you whether or not you should get a tattoo. That's your fucking body, do with it what you want. I do suggest, though, that before you put that permanent ink on your body, think long and hard! Tattoos are not a game, unless they are the ones you get out of a Cracker Jack box, the ones you lick and press on your arm. Actually, I'm not even sure if they put them in there anymore, I like Crunch 'n Munch. Those tattoos wash off with soap and water; a real tattoo needs a fucking laser to get it off, and even when it comes off it leaves a mark to remind you of the stupid mistake you made one drunken night in Cabo.

Look, you get a rose or some Chinese symbol, what can I say, that's what you wanted. Obviously you need to make sure you know what the Chinese symbol means in English 'cause trust me, if I was tattooing and I knew you hadn't taken the time to look shit up, you had best know I would write some dumb shit on your lower back, ladies. Shit like—*My Other Car Is a Benz*, *If You Can Read This You're Too Close*, or *My Kid Is on the Honor Roll*. You know, stupid shit like that. Crazy damn MILF!

The real danger lies when you start tattooing names on your body. If you tattoo your own name, you're safe—egotistical . . . possibly forgetful—but safe. It's when your dumb, hopeful ass tattoos the name of someone you're dating, that's when you're looking for trouble. You have to be careful when you tattoo your significant other's name on you because if you break up, you're going to spend the rest of your life either:

1. looking for someone with that name;
2. looking for someone who is okay with seeing another person's name on you because they are into threesomes;
3. looking for someone else dumb enough to have someone else's name on them.

Bottom line: Tattoos are permanent! That shit costs hundreds of dollars to remove and it's painful!

Now, I get that some tattoos are sexy, but why not enjoy the same look by just purchasing a box of washable markers? I'm telling you, get some, get with your significant other, and doodle on each other! That's sexy as shit! Draw hearts and stars, and if you want to get creative, write sexy things like *Enter here, No shirts, no service,* or my personal favorite, *Backing up can cause severe tire damage!* And here's another fun option: Doodle some ants all over your lady. When she looks at them, just tell her the ants are attacking her. When she asks you why, you tell her it's because she's so sweet! Ladies love shit like that!

I can hear some of you screaming that I don't get it, that one of the main points of tattooing is that it is permanent. That it's a commitment. Really? Is that what you're saying? You're hard core like that?! Sorry, but I'm not impressed by some dumb ass tattooing *Tracy* on the back of his neck only to break up with Tracy three months later. You wanna impress me? Don't tattoo her name on you, tattoo her whole damn body on you! A life-size tattoo! Have a tattoo that starts just under your chin and goes all the way down to your feet. It should be a tattoo of the back of her lying on the front of you. You get what the hell I'm saying? I want it so that when you're lying on your back, that tattoo looks like your lady is lying on top of you! Now that's a damn permanent ass tattoo! Shit, if I ever was to get one, though, I would get something that is useful, like a tattoo of pockets on both my hips with money coming out of them—that way I'd always have cash on me. Tat-heads, don't steal that one.

BALLS AND CHAINS

Before you get married, find out if you got yourself an all-inclusive partner. Do you know what that is? That's a partner who offers all the perks! You see, getting married is like taking a long ass cruise, and if you know anything about cruises, it's very important that you know what's included—before that damn ship sails! And a wedding is like when that ship leaves: If you wait till after it's at sea to find what you've got, you may want to jump overboard and drown yourself somewhere in the Pacific.

If you have determined that your partner is an all-inclusive, first of all, good for you: all-inclusive ain't easy to come by! The next thing you will need to do right before your ass gets married is to sign some REAL VOW documents. I'm talking about the shit you don't talk about when you exchange marriage vows. They include a contract and a waiver. The contract is for *One Freak Night of Sexual Activity a Week* and the waiver is *Against Injury Incurred During Said Freaky Night*—injuries such as Rug Burn (occurring either to the knees or crotch), Headboard Knot (occurring on the lady's head as a result of pounding against the headboard), or Double Whammy (occurring when an intense session causes both).

With the agreements in place, it's on to the actual day. Now, on that big day, I know it's part of some old ass tradition, but I'm telling you now: Don't let anyone in the room be called the "best man." You're the best man! You're the groom, right? You have the nicest suit on, right? The bride picked you, right? So you're the best damn man in that room! If I ever get married, I'm going to be my own best man.

See, the bride doesn't even try to mess with some bullshit like that! A lady would never let her best friend be called the "best woman"! What?!? There ain't no way that damn bride is gonna have some woman running around her wedding, claiming to be the best woman! As a matter of fact, the bride makes sure her friend knows what time it is by calling her the "maid of honor." A fucking *maid*—that's some control shit, but I can't argue with it. I say take a hint from the bride and call the best man the "butler of honor." And then, just to make sure that neither one of them steals either of your shine, let the two of them fuck each other's brains out in the bathroom while you schmooze your guests and eat all the overpriced catering that everyone is complaining about behind your back anyway. Remember, this is *your* fucking day!

All things being equal, people should always elope. Don't get me wrong: Go have fun planning, tasting cakes, and trying on shiny outfits. Hell, even set a date and send out invites. But when the time comes, you and your bride grab a ladder, climb out some window, and elope. Leave those stupid ass guests sitting there waiting for you! They will thank you! You think they want to be there?! Nobody wants to go to some dumb ass reception, eat terrible food, and dance with people from five different age groups. When you elope, you solve all those problems, plus you give your guests some gossip to bitch about! People love to gossip and talk shit about bad weddings!

If you can't tell, I hate going to weddings! Most of the ones I've been to should not have happened, and I knew it. I bet you've wanted to stop a wedding or two in your day—I bet most people have. Problem is, people are too scared to speak up when the preacher asks if anyone sees a reason why these two should not be joined in holy matrimony blah blah blah . . . Me? I'm not scared of shit! I will stop a wedding! I'll bring one to a dead halt! I'll stop it for dumb shit, too. One time, I objected because the bride and groom both had weird ass shapes—they were both top-heavy! See, that shit could never work! As I have mentioned earlier, people are like Lego pieces: They need to fit together, literally! If one is top-heavy, the other needs to be bottom heavy so that they can interlock while fucking!

I'm surprised more weddings don't get stopped, because that's too much damn power to give an audience! Imagine if they gave audiences on Broadway that power. Imagine how many times plays would get stopped with some muthafucka wanting a refund! *Wicked, Grease, Hamilton!?!*

Imagine that! Fucking *Hamilton*! You bought some tickets two years ago and patiently waited for the night of your ticket date to roll around. Finally that day comes, you get dressed up, get a babysitter, and head over to the theater. You get there, sit in one of those tiny 1920s Broadway seats, and you get excited as the lights go down. All of a sudden, the cast of *Hamilton* is rapping. You stare in disbelief at the people around you. You are shocked. You hate rap, and you damn sure didn't know that they would be rapping the whole damn thing! You sit there and take about as much as you can handle, and halfway through the show you object! Now they got to stop the show. Then the police come and tackle you, but you run onstage and grab a musket from one of the actors—'cause that's what they used in Hamilton's day—and you try to shoot it out, all cause you have the right to object!

And now because of your bullshit decision you have the right to an attorney. By the way, I heard that *Hamilton* is fucking amazing. I got to try to sneak in to see it one day, unless someone out there has a plus one.

WIFE INSURANCE

One thing to consider before you enter any sort of marital commitment is wife insurance. Now, before you get started on me, this is NOT a sexist concept. I'm not going to serve you some outdated cliché saying that in every divorce the woman wants to clean the man out. I know firsthand there are plenty of kick ass women out there who are either taking care of a bunch of kids all by themselves because some weak-minded man dipped out on them or, worse than that, have to dole out spousal support to some punk ass ex-husbands.

But the fact is, men are DISORGANIZED. When a woman gets a divorce, she has a backup plan. She has saved up money for a rainy day, maybe at Wells Fargo, maybe in the Cayman Islands—point is, she has a plan. She has already made a bid on her exciting new home or booked a long-term luxurious Airbnb with a Cuban pool boy included. Not to mention that smart ass woman has backup dicks stashed all over the state and in offshore locations. That's how women handle their business. Men? Men get divorced with no plan and no money, and they wind up depressed in some old raggedy motel, or back home with their parents, or, worse yet, in the basement of their own damn house.

Imagine if these fuck-ups had a secret wife insurance policy waiting to pay them off so that they could enjoy their new single status in style. It would take into account all the needs a divorced man has. Shit like helping him find a new place to live—or maybe even a sexy, compassionate cougar with a PhD in psychology to help him deal with his devastating sense of loneliness and depression—would be covered. It would help that lonely, dumb ass man get over his trauma and issues so he could attract a better mate the next time around. And it would cover date coaching, weight-loss coaching, and, most important, erection coaching. A premium package would also cover sex costs for the first seven days, although for now that option would be available only in the state of Nevada.

Needless to say, the wife insurance policy would have strict terms that would cause pre-existing conditions to disqualify you from collecting (see the section in the book covering flu dick). Also, if this is your second/third/fourth time around, the premium would be adjusted accordingly. I mean, did you not learn anything? To determine your risk, the adjusters would interview your crazy ass exes, your alcoholic grandma, and the nice girl who would have given you a hand job if you didn't fucking open your big mouth about being married in the first place. In other words, for example, car insurance companies are not going to pay you if you steal your own fucking car. Take note.

ESCAPE CLAUSE

𝔍 don't want to piss off the ladies, so I'm going to open with a disclaimer: I'm a man. I bring the ruckus to the ladies. I have a black belt in fucking. And so I will be writing this section from a man's perspective. Just like I mentioned when I was talking to you about wife insurance, we men are the ones who need divorce advice because women are fucking communicative. When they are not happy, they just wake up one morning and tell their shit-for-nothing husband, "I'm done." Or, "I've been fucking the Columbian housepainter the last four months, and it has been fantastic."

Many of you fools are unhappy in your marriage and you are dying for a divorce, but you're too scared to say it. Now, some men will never have this problem because they are the type of guys who, when they get bored in the relationship, start cheating. And whether they mean to be or not, they are so sloppy with their cheating that they get caught and their relationship ends. Problem, though, for some of you is that you're not the kind of devious type who would cheat on your wife. And look, there's nothing wrong with devious types—I mean, they are often contractors, own nightclubs, or even sell used cars, so they do contribute to society. But for the rest of you nondevious types, I have a better, more passive-aggressive technique that will lead you to the desired result without having to engage in that shady shit. I mean, come on, don't disrespect women. Suppose that was your sister? Or your mother? I wish you would try and cheat on my mother; I would whup your ass! Here is my four-step break-up technique:

1. **Contact Replacement/Renaming:** A first easy step is to replace the most frequently used contacts on your phone with hot lady names. Include Natasha, Coco, and Peaches, no typical shit. Friends can be enlisted to actually role-play if your lady chooses to call and confront them. Now, if your wife is not the jealous type, or if she's very trusting, then the phone shit won't work. Time to kick it up a notch.

2. **Controlled Nightmares:** Natasha, Coco, and Peaches will now appear in your dreams. How dirty those dreams get is entirely up to you, because you will be yelling out shit in the middle of the night while pretending to be asleep. If you're a great performer and can be convincingly vocal, do your dizzle and go for fucking gold. Just don't overdo the volume, 'cause that can make the shit sound unbelievable, plus if you've got thin ass walls you'll just sound crazy to your kids and/or neighbors.

3. **Staging a "Real" Affair without Actually Fucking:** If, for some crazy ass reason, Wifey finds your fuck fantasies amusing and still can't imagine you would ever actually cheat on her . . . then you're clearly rockin' a cornball image in her eyes, which is a whole other problem we don't have time to entertain right now. So anyway, at this point, cornball, you're really gonna have to go for it. Again, I'm not saying you actually go fuck around ('cause that's not gonna help your ass in the divorce settlement, unless you're into losing your shit, 'cause that shit could happen) but making her *believe you are* will get the results you need. Yes, she will hate your ass, but that will HELP her move the fuck

on. Her level of hatred, resentment, and disgust will cause her
to leave you. Trust me, you'll be doing her a favor. She'll feel so
empowered by leaving you that she will be able to hang out with
her friends, sip her glass of chardonnay (women love that wine
shit), and tell them that she got out in time and didn't waste the
rest of her life with that asshole Kelvin!

4. **The Leon Phase:** Some crazy ass women refuse to give up on
the marriage no matter what happens. They could walk in on
you fucking their best friend, but after they scream and throw
some bowls and cutlery around, they will sit down with you
and suggest couples therapy (Fuck!) so BOTH of you can take
responsibility and figure out how you got into this dark place to
begin with. Who has time for that shit? If that setback happens,
I, Leon, will intervene. You text me, I will come over, take your
lady to the bedroom, and bring so much ruckus she won't have
any desire to see your cornball ass ever again.

RAISING
KIDS

NAME DAT BABY

𝔍t took me a long time to embrace the name "Leon." Now, I know some of you are thinking, "How about Leo, Leon?" First of all, I wish a muthfucka would call me "Leo!" I would knock somebody out for some lazy ass shit like that! That would be like calling Larry "Lar." Why the fuck would you do that? Larry is already short for Lawrence! Why the fuck would you short a short! No, you can only short a short with certain names. Like someone says, "Hey, my name is William, but you can call me Willy for short!" Then you can short that short by calling Willy "Will"! See, that shit is cool: You have a formal name for dinner parties and job interviews and a casual name for clubs and arrest reports. Now that I think about it, you can also call that muthafucka Bill. Fuck William—bad example!

Or how about Richard: You can call that muthafucka Rich or—get this—Dick! Where the fuck did Dick come from!?! That's why I say take your time when you're coming up with a name for your damn seed. Don't get caught up with no trends like naming kids nature shit, like River or Sky; and unless you want to raise a stripper, stay away from alcoholic beverages like Courvoisier, Brandy, or Sex on the Beach; shit like that ends badly.

Here are some important factors that go into choosing a good ass name that won't fuck your kid up for life:

1. Don't choose a name until your kid is at least five years old. Until then, just keep alternating names to see which one fits. This will confuse your kid, but eventually none of those names will have any meaning to that kid. Eventually, he or she will respond to anything without caring, which is exactly what you want. You want to build a kid who's not sensitive to the nonsense around them. That way bullies with all the mean shit they say will have no power against that kid.

2. Also, don't choose that name too early, because to be honest, I know that's your kid, but you don't know that kid yet! You have no idea what your kid's personality is gonna be like, and the last thing you want to do is give your kid some punk ass name like Kyle when it becomes clear, when he turns sixteen, that he should've been a Dwayne.

3. Stop trying to be so damn original. It's a global world out there, and you want to make sure your name sounds powerful no matter where you are. Names that might be good in one area might not translate somewhere else. Make shit sound like it spells and make it easy to pronounce. Like, what if you've given your daughter some beautiful African name like Nyla and she ends up falling in love with some Japanese businessman, but her husband can't pronounce that shit and she has to live her entire life with her name being slaughtered by her own fucking husband.

4. I know #3 sounds racist, but it's the truth: Some ethnicities have a hard time pronouncing words that other cultures say with no trouble. For instance, Larry let me try some nasty-looking food that he likes, and I'll be damned if I didn't fall in love with that shit. Problem is, I can't pronounce it, so whenever I want some of

it, I tell Larry, "Lemme get some of that good ass nasty shit," and he knows exactly what I'm talking about.

5. Every random ass new word you hear does not necessarily make for a good baby name. Don't be some dude who overhears some woman on a train talking about her labia and then run home and tell the mother of your unborn baby that you want to name it that . . . don't do that! Look up a word before you use it, let alone name your kid it. Don't make your lady have to point out to you just how dumb you are. Or, worse yet, don't have that kid get fucked up in the end because both of her parents were dumb enough to think Labia would be a good damn name.

HARD HEAD—
SOFT BEHIND

'all are prisoners, prisoners of convention. You dole out cash to your kid for every stupid, cavity-ridden tooth that falls out. I mean, what the fuck? Have you forgotten that *you* are the Tooth Fairy, *you* are the Easter Bunny, *you* are that jolly ass Santa! Wake up! *You* establish the market and you make the rules. Instead of candy, give your kids vitamins; instead of money, give them a washcloth and soap. And if your alcoholic mother still wants to give them money, you take that dollar and tear it in half, and take that damn half a dollar and put it under your kid's pillow so that when they wake up and see it, they will have to ask themselves, "What did I do wrong?" Doesn't matter that they didn't do anything wrong, they *think* they did, and the guilt and fear makes them manageable. It fucks with their head and prepares them for life. And that is good parenting.

There's an emotional song I enjoy listening to, I don't remember the name but I love the fuck out of the song. That being said, there are some lyrics that I feel are misleading. For instance, "I believe the children are our future . . ." That lyric single-handedly fucked up parenting. Also, "Show them the beauty they possess inside . . ." Beauty should be obvious. Something that has to be shown is not. And let's be honest, most kids are not beautiful inside, they're just rotten. I'm not saying it's always the kid's fault, but it's simple math. If every other piece of fruit in the house is rotten, how do you think that little ass tangerine is gonna turn out?

Really, parenting begins right when that damn baby pops out! If that doctor doesn't slap that ass good, things will never be right. Next big moment is feeding that damn baby. Now, I was a breast baby myself, and that's the best way to go. Canned milk is all right, but it ain't as good as breast milk. "Why did I say 'breast milk' instead of 'titty milk'?" you ask. Because breast milk is for the baby and titty milk is for the daddy . . . if you're into that kind of thing. Now, back to breast milk versus canned milk: Don't get me wrong, although breast milk is better, you can still fuck your kid up with that stuff 'cause you have to know when to get your kid off the titty. See, I said "titty" there, because when that breast turns back into a titty, it's time to get that damn kid off it! I saw a documentary where this lady was still titty feeding her eight-year-old kid, and she was having trouble weaning him off. As a matter of fact, she said she started trying to get him to stop when he was five. Hell, at five that little muthafucka was already too old! Mothers, you want a tip on how to wean your baby (or in some cases your husband or boyfriend) off the titty? Hot sauce! I had a friend that said his mother got him to stop sucking his thumb by putting hot sauce on it. I suggest you put some hot sauce on your nipple, but make sure to put some Vaseline on first so you don't burn your shit. Trust me, when whoever goes in for a sweet sip gets hit with that red-hot taste, the suck session will be over.

One disclaimer: If you're dating someone black, the hot sauce might not be a deterrent. I'm just saying.

IT TAKES A DAMN VILLAGE

𝕴 hate tired ass phrases that don't mean shit. For instance, "Look at you." What's the point of that one? Can you reeeally look at yourself? I do think it would be great if you could actually see yourself. You do realize, though, that most people in your life have seen you more than you have seen you. I mean, you've seen yourself in mirrors and pictures and shit, but to be honest, when it's all said and done, you have never really seen yourself enough to know what you really look like. Like if you could somehow walk behind yourself, trust me, you would be like, "Who is this dumb muthafucka in front of me?"

Think about it: When you dream, you create a little image of you in there. It's a version of you that you think is accurate. But if you could ever let someone you know drop by one of your dreams for a cameo, they would look at that little dream you and be like, "Who the fuck is that?" And you would be like, "Me," and they would be like, "That's not what the fuck you look like." At which point you would probably dream a ferocious cougar into the scenario to eat your friend's ass for talking shit. Regardless, you don't really know what the fuck you look like.

Or another one is like when people say it takes a village. I get it, you're saying everyone should play their part in raising that kid. By the way, I would actually prefer to say it takes a village to raise "children," but I acknowledge it doesn't sound right. Personally I just don't like the word "kid." A "kid" is a goat, so in reality, you're saying it takes a village to raise a goat, which doesn't make any damn sense. Oh, and don't be shocked that I knew "kid" is another name for "goat." To be honest, I would be shocked if you didn't know. And if you didn't, now would be a good time to look at yourself and see *why* you didn't know. See how I brought that shit back around?

Back to the whole "village to raise your kids" bullshit: You know how many strong single moms and dads I've met? Ones that have raised several kids!?! Who the hell came up with that saying? My thing is, what the hell is wrong with that kid? You think that village ain't got nothing better to do? How about running businesses, driving Ubers, hustling and bustling? Is the village supposed to just stop what they're doing to raise that mess of a kid? Where are his parents? I tell you, what that village needs to do, they need to line them parents up and whup their asses for trying to pawn off their parenting responsibilities on the damn village! A village got shit to do, shit like putting horseshoes on horses, paying taxes to the king, and burning witches . . .

Maybe I went back too far, but you get the idea—raise your own fucking kids!

BIRDS AND BEES

And while we're on the subject of bullshit phrases, here's an expression that drives me crazy: Why is it that when a parent wants to talk to their children about sex, they use that stupid old "birds and bees" thing? First thing motherfucking first, a bird would never fuck a bee. You would never see that shit. They'd both get hurt. Birds like birds and bees like bees; if anything a bird might eat a bee, but he wouldn't fuck it. Plain and simple, birds eat bees!

If anything, if you want to use the birds and bees phrase in a productive way, use it to inspire your kids to try a new trade! Give your kids a beekeeper suit—you know how much natural honey costs? Or how about a falcon and one of them falconry gloves? Let your kid take that to school. I bet your kid will never get bullied with a big ass falcon on his arm! Just make sure to consider your kid's weight when choosing the size of your falcon, because they can and most definitely will carry a small child away. I've seen it happen.

Really, when you think about it, why would someone ever have come up with having "the birds and bees talk"? If you ask me, that's just some random shit! They might as well have called it "the potatoes and onions talk"! Now, that one would have made more sense! Just like how the birds and the bees are different, so are potatoes and onions, but at least you can picture potatoes and onions hooking up. I mean, on the one hand you've got this strange shape, bulky ass–looking potato man hooking up with a multilayered sweet yet pungent lady onion! And we all know what happens when a potato hooks up with an onion: home fries. See? That makes sense.

I do realize, though, at the core of that sloppy ass metaphor is the real issue of how do you talk to your kids about sex. Look here, it's an important conversation, and I can't state it enough that it's not a time to fuck around with metaphors. Trust me, when your teenager brings home that newborn baby, that metaphor will turn into reality very fast. To me, the way you deal with it is the same way you get into a cold ass pool: You dive the fuck in and deal with the initial shock. Just walk up to your kid, look him/her in the eye, and say, "Speaking of fucking!" Once you start there and the shock wears off, everything will be much easier to talk about.

To be honest, I don't believe in long bullshit conversations to explain fucking to your kids. Just like the expression "It's easier to ask for forgiveness than permission," I say the best way to go is to just let your kid catch you a few times. Trust me, it's easier to explain to them what the fuck they just saw than to explain to them what the fuck is supposed to happen.

RAN-AWAYS

The runaway epidemic has gotten out of control, for one reason only: You can't tell who's a runaway anymore. Years ago people dressed based on their social class: You knew who was rich and who was poor, who was black and who was white. These days, everyone dresses the same way: raggedy. A runaway? You can't spot a runaway when they are interspersed among the motherfucking hipsters and hobos.

Another one often confused for a runaway is a hitchhiker, but they are pretty easy to distinguish. First of all, a hitchhiker is too old to be running away. Second, while a runaway is running away, a hitchhiker is more likely on the run; that's a big difference. You run away from shit like your parents or school; you are on the run from shit like the authorities or your responsibilities. Plus a runaway is the one you wonder, "Where the fuck did they come from!?!" And the hitchhiker is the one you wonder, "Where the fuck are they going!?!"

See, back in the day, a runaway was the one roaming around holding that long branch over their shoulder with the pouch on the end. Runaways are pretty hard to catch because they can scamper like mothafuckas. As for that pouch, it would be made out of some polka dot bandanna and it would be filled with loose change, underwear, and a peanut butter and jelly sandwich. Shit like that is easy to spot. You would go to a Greyhound station and see that kid with that damn branch, immediately you would be like, "Someone grab that damn runaway!"

Or if you've just gotten off a plane and you're waiting for your ugly ass suitcase by the baggage carousel, and you see that long ass branch with a satchel at the end of it, you know that runaway is gonna come claim that. So you just wait for that runaway. And when a barefoot kid with overalls, freckles, and buck teeth walks over to claim his fucking stick with the goddamn pouch, you know that's your fucking runaway. And you get his ass home. Put him on the next flight to Pig, Tennessee. Real place, I got stuck there once, ended up tappin' some ass. Shout to Shirley—thanks for the pie!

MANAGING
MONEY

IN ME I TRUST

$\mathcal{A}$lthough the name of this section is "Managing Money," trust me, very little of it will have anything to do with actually handling and or investing money. Now, I *could* give you advice and it would probably be damn good, but when it comes down to it, I think instead of giving you financial advice I would rather advise you on who to take financial advice from. Take me, for example: I don't have any damn money—I'm not poor, mind you, I'm rich in many ways. Hell, I live in a beautiful house and drive around in a fancy car; neither of them is mine, but trust me, I'm living well. That being said, on paper and in my pocket, I don't have any money. Point number one: Don't take money advice from someone who doesn't have money. I don't think I have to explain that one. And my second and final point: Don't take financial advice from people who teach seminars by the airport. Those shady muthafuckas get you into some damn Sheraton conference room, offer you some cookies and water, and promise you that if you buy their book you'll have their secret to getting rich. Well, I'll let you in on the secret for free: They got rich by selling their book.

Look, I can't have a chapter like this and not give you any money ad-vice, so here's one tip: Learn how to talk about your money like rich people do. Rich people don't use terms that precisely label the amount of money they have, they use ones that make a little sound like a lot. "Five hundred thousand dollars" may sound like a lot of money, but "half a million" sounds like way more. Don't believe me? Maybe that's because you're poor.

Okay, I'll put it in terms that your poor ass can understand: I'm sure you could buy a few things with five hundred dollars, but just imagine how much you could buy with half a thousand dollars. See?!?

WALKAWAY PLAN

S tyle is very important to me. A lot of people will tell you that you need a lot of money to be stylish, but there are creative ways around it. And before you get it twisted, I'm not telling you to steal! As a matter of fact, I hate a thief! There are many ways to get along in life without fucking people over. I call it "The Come Up!" The Come Up is a way to keep things moving; for football fans, its like *moving the chains*, or moving your life down the field. You don't have to go for a touchdown on every play, you just wanna keep getting first downs. It's when you get greedy that you end up fumbling and that's when you get arrested and wind up in jail. You wanna make sure you have a solid game plan for your life. You do what you gotta do, till you can do what you wanna do! Shit, I should put that shit on a fucking t-shirt.

Now, I don't know how many of you are familiar with the term "layaway." That was this thing back in the day where you could buy some shit from the store and pay it off over time like the way you would do a car or a house, only you could buy a hat or some drawers that way. They don't do that type of shit anymore, but I tell you what, *I do*. I call my plan "Walkaway." See what I do is I buy myself an outfit, keep them tags on, tuck that shit in, and wear it as much I want. If someone happens to see the tags, I just pretend I forgot to take them off. Then when I get tired of that outfit, I go back to the store wearing that same outfit and exchange it for something else, then I *walk away* with my nice new outfit. See, it's not stealing if you're just exchanging.

MAN-MADE

The Amish have it right. Simple living. Making your own butter. That's the shit. But I don't want to make my own butter. Butter is cheap and good and comes in a stick, so I like it. What I wanna do is learn how to make my own cereal. 'Cause the cereal makers keep that shit secret. It's fucking frustrating. I mean, if McDonald's can tell you how to make a Big Mac, why can't Procter & Gamble tell me how to make Cap'n Crunch? I'll tell you, because it's fucking impossible to make. You ever read what's in it?! All those additives and preservatives!? The average person doesn't have the scientific ability to do it!

Not only that, but cereal is fucking expensive. Cap'n Crunch is like six dollars a box!?!?! That's more than a gallon of gasoline! Why does a box of damn cereal cost more than a gallon of gasoline?! For six dollars a box, it should come with milk and a spoon already in there! And a divider in the box to keep that shit from getting messy.

Here's the rub: If you do figure out how to make your own cereal, you will fuck the market up. That's why the cereal makers are so fucking scared. That's why they keep the Froot Loops recipe under such wraps.

But guess what? I don't want to make fucking Froot Loops or Cap'n

Crunch. I want to make adult cereal. 'Cause adults are the ones stuck with the boring ass cereals like Special K and Chex. We need to spice that shit up.

I'm making a cereal called "Junk Drawer." That would be one of those surprise cereals, 'cause you never know what you have in your fucking junk drawer. So all the pieces of cereal would be shaped accordingly. Edible shit, only shaped like a toenail clipper, gummy bear, scissors, chopsticks, soy sauce packets, spare keys. And the box would be shaped like a drawer, and you don't open it from the top—the compartment just slides out like a real drawer.

"Kitty Litter" is also a good name for a cereal. It just sounds good. It's not about what it is, it's about what it's made of. It's still good and sweet. And you put a cute ass kitten on the box? Boom! People love fucking kittens! You will sell that shit. Throw some chocolate chunks in there to keep it real. Even better, put a Hawaiian shirt and shorts on the kitty. Everyone loves a Hawaiian kitty. Everyone loves Hawaiian everything!

How much better would the homeless look if we gave them all Hawaiian shirts and flip-flops?

Maybe we can also create a homeless cereal that's a little cheaper, easier to digest, and feeds them through the day. Better yet, let's make a cereal called "Windfall." The pieces are shaped like coins. Fucking brilliant. Fuck that. Let's go forward backward and make all coins edible. That way people can either use it or eat it. The government's gotta make more money anyway. That way the people who don't have a meal at home can eat their salary, so if they ate like pigs, they can just spend it on some hookers and blow if they choose. If you go to IHOP and order silver-dollar pancakes, they're gonna be made out of actual silver dollars, so you can eat one and pay for it with another.

If you're a family of five and all you have is a ten-dollar bill, you go get change for that ten dollars and then you can feed the whole table. Economy fixed. Hunger fixed.

Homemade is not always a good thing. Sure, someone invites your ass over for some homemade apple pie, that's a good thing. But what if they offer you a stick of homemade gum? No good. Don't take any homemade thing that you can't make yourself! Shit like gum! And aspirin! Cereal! Fucking deodorant! You mean to tell me you're at home making deodorant? You somehow figure out the "musty code," wise ass? No way, muthafucka. No way you are making homemade deodorant that actually works. And don't even think of telling me it's antiperspirant, because I know the difference between the two and I'm not risking my sex life on your homemade lab experiments.

DINE AND DITCH, BITCH

I don't fuck with the gourmet shit. I watch shows about survival types of food. Living extravagantly is a pain in the ass. When you live extravagantly, you gotta spend a lot of time skipping out on the goddamn bill; you got to be the guy who goes to the bathroom and climbs out the window. But the gourmet food makes you fat and shit, and your hips get too wide to crawl out of the fucking window.

When skipping out on the bill, you can opt for the tried-and-true diarrhea excuse, especially if you hate the people you just had dinner with. (If they're really annoying, make sure you flourish with runny, juicy, explosive, and smelly farts.) Other options include court cases and pregnancies, but if you want to keep it simple, a nosebleed is the way to go. Always carry a hankie with that red dye shit. You come out holding that hankie to your nose (don't overtilt your head back), then shake your head, like you're confused and shit. "Leon, what happened?" Now, DO NOT give a specific answer, 'cause then you'll ruin your chance to repeat this technique.

Just keep shaking your head.

"I don't know. I don't know."

"You gotta see a doctor, man."

"I will. I will."

You can pull the "I will" excuse two or three more times, but at some point, you're gonna have to throw in "I'm seeing a doctor next Thursday." (Always use Thursday—it's the most believable day of the week.)

The bloody-nose technique can get you out of numerous situations. Like if you're with a lady and you're gonna come too quick, get that ejackalit out into the world, then pull out the hankie. There are some people who do suffer from chronic nosebleeds. I envy those muthafuckas. Their nose is like a blood faucet that can't be turned off. Those fuckers can donate blood through their nose. They don't have to deal with goddamn needles. They just stroll into the blood clinic, open their nose, and then enjoy the orange juice and goddamn cookie. 'Cause why else would you donate blood except to get that juice and yummy cookie?

ALWAYS BET ON BLACK

Listen, it's a known fact: Parents are always tight-fisted when it comes to money. Grandparents are a bit easier, and great-grandparents (if you can find some alive) are even easier. Old people are just more generous with their money and are easier to get over on.

That's why, when I walk into a casino, I don't see slot machines, I see family members. I seek out the old ones, the grandparents and the great-grandparents, with a few old ass uncles thrown in. I know that those cats are gonna be eager for thrills and not as concerned with their remaining account balances. If you can find a grandpa who's estranged from his son, even better. Those cats get rid of their cash on purpose just to spite their ungrateful kids.

Once you spot these old people, you slide on in there like the grandkid they never had. You compliment them on their clothing, their perfume or cologne, you talk to them about shit they can relate to, like Efferdent. You tell them you wish your grandparents were still alive and then get them talking about *their* grandparents. By the end of it, they are so emotional they just sit there and let you win. They give you more money to "Go have some fun!" and "Buy yourself an ice cream to boot."

Personally, I stay away from the new Vegas shit: too many bells and whistles to distract me from the task at hand. I don't need to pretend I'm in Paris and eat some French ass bread shipped in from Reno. If I'm in Vegas, I'll hit the old stinky places, like Circus Circus. That place smells like cig-arettes and ejackalit from the 1960s. It's still on their damn carpet. They're just too underfunded to get proper sanitation equipment or to refurbish. You find old cats in there, you know they're alone, 'cause if they were on good terms with their family they'd all be at the Venetian, riding around in a gondola with some Dominican dude pretending to know Italian.

The best casinos are the ones right outside of Vegas, about twenty miles out. Like Primm and Jean, Nevada. Those places house the real ad-dicts. The people who can't wait to actually get to Vegas to gamble, they pull over twenty miles out—not to fill up on gas or get some soda; they go in so they can gamble their money away as soon as fucking possible. Those are the real addicts. Those places are hard core and give you the real gam-bling vibe if you want it.

'Cause let me tell you something: Vegas is like a beautiful lady who won't give you a good time. You want to find the ugly people, because ugly people try harder.

IKEA PARTIES

Some people think this implies having a party where people come over to help you build all the shit you bought at IKEA. There are endless party rooms to choose from based on the type of party you're throwing. You've got kitchens and dining rooms for nice dinner parties. You can serve little finger foods, some wine in fancy wineglasses; they've got all that shit there. Nothing with sauces or gravies, no sloppy shit—remember, there's no water to clean shit up. Of course, you have living rooms for casual get-togethers and bedrooms if you want to have some light, swinger-type stuff. Ain't nothing wrong with that. Plenty of comfortable seating. A cleanup staff. Just make sure to specify what room you are using, 'cause otherwise your guests are gonna get sucked into the marketplace section buying placemats and cutlery and related shit for the dancing.

Note: If any of your guests try and show with a bunch of Swedish meatballs from the IKEA cafeteria instead of bringing some tasty shit from home, send them to the warehouse section for punishment.

HOMELESS DEPOT

The other day I was riding past Home Depot and I saw a lot of what're called "day workers" standing out in front, trying to hustle some handyman gigs. Now, I can't speak for everyone out there, but I assume that most of them are either poor, homeless, or both. Now don't get me wrong: It's quite possible that a few of them could be some of those crazy ass rich people who either like to see how the other half lives or have lost their minds and have like $1.2 million in nickels hidden in a storm drain at their house. Anyway, I was thinking about those poor souls who need a place to stay and are willing to work hard, and all of a sudden it hit me!

Home Depot is an amazing place—you got fifty aisles and a garden center in that shit. Now, what the government should do is subsidize housing by buying Home Depots and allowing homeless people to build their own houses *inside* the Home Depot, 'cause they got all the necessary materials in there already! Wood, hammers, dishwashers, BBQ equipment. They can even grow their own food in the garden department. It would be the *Homeless Depot*! It's a house within a house within a fucking house.

Once all the houses are built, every aisle would be a new

neighborhood—better yet, a development. And the shit is gated, so it's basically a gated community, with ample fucking parking. Tell me that's not a good ass idea! But I do recommend getting rid of the shopping carts: They tend to attract homeless people, and that would just bring you back to square one.

JEHOVAH WITNESS PROTECTION PROGRAM

N ow, apart from the homeless, who for the most part have had some fucked-up circumstance and find themselves in unfortunate situations, I want to shine some light on another group of people. A group of people who also find themselves homeless, but this group did that shit to themselves and now expect other people to take care of them and pay their way. I'm talking about muthafuckas in the Witness Protection Program!

You see them in movies all the time cutting deals and getting set up somewhere nice. And who pays for that!? Taxpayers, that's who! And why? I mean, *you* fucked up! Why should I pay for you to get some nice house in Phoenix! Fucking 5346 Canyon Drive in Phoenix, with that nice ass view, just 'cause somebody wants to blow your fucking head off because you squealed on Two Finger Tony for some racketeering charge, huh, Mike? You, your wife, your two beautiful kids, your fucking mother-in-law? That's on you, Mike! (Hypothetically speaking, of course.)

I tell you what the courts or the feds or whoever is cutting that deal should do: Make them work that shit off!

Fuck it, send them to work for the Jehovah Witness knocking on doors and handing out pamphlets and shit. Being with them is like being hidden in plain sight! You could show up at someone's door with blood on your jacket, handcuffs on, racketeering money hanging out of your pocket and be wearing an *I Snitch* t-shirt, and still no one would make the connection. Believe me, nobody is looking to find anyone associated with the Jehovah Witness! Perfect hiding place! Now you could hook them up with Scientology, but I would only do that in cases of extreme deep cover. Actually I have the perfect job for them! Since people in the Witness Protection Program can't show their faces, make them team mascots. You know those dumb ass costumed ones you see at games, like that green big-bottomed one, the Phillie Phanatic, or the San Diego Chicken, or even the one from New York with that big baseball head—shit, even those damn big ass sausages that race. You ever see those sausages? I think one is a kielbasa, one is Italian, one is Polish, I think there's even a racist-looking chorizo wearing a sombrero—anyway, those muthafuckas race and it's hilarious!

Anyway, they don't get to be anything cool like that because those mascots fuck. Trust me, people wait for them till after the game to play out some fantasies and fuck. Think that San Diego Chicken—as long as he has been doing it—doesn't have a bunch of baby chicks running around? Like I said, don't let them be cool ones at major sporting events, make them work at bullshit parks in the middle of nowhere. And make sure the character they play is real degrading: Make them dress up in a gigantic ass costume, one with two big buttocks! And make sure the team has a Foot in the Ass Day, where fans get to come on the field and kick the Ass! That's what you get, Mike!

GETTING OVER AND GETTING AHEAD

SLOW THE FUCK UP

This one is easy: In life, don't rush your shit! Take your time, 'cause when you don't trust me, you will fuck up! Unless a safe has fallen from a window and is about to drop on your head, take your time! Watch how easy I explain this to you!

When McDonald's has their 99-cent Big Mac sale, right, people love the fuckin' Big Mac. But because it's 99 cents, everybody wants 'em, right? People order four, five at a time. But now, the people who work there gotta rush. They gotta fuckin' rush to make the fuckin' Big Mac faster, because everybody wants 'em. They're fucking 99 cents! But now they've fuckin' rushed them so fuckin' fast that every once in a while you bite into a Big Mac and it's missing one of the goddamn ingredients! Everybody knows it's two all-beef patties, special sauce, lettuce, cheese, pickles, onions, on a sesame seed bun, right? You fuck around and bite one of them Big Macs that's missing special sauce, you're like, "Fuck! There's no special sauce on this muthafucka!" You bite another one, the pickles ain't in the shit. You know why? Because muthafuckas is rushing. It takes time. You gotta make the shit how it's supposed to be made. When you start rushing the burger, you open the shit up—the burger's crooked and shit. What the fuck? The burger's hanging halfway off the goddamn bun, because they're fuckin' rushing, and they're not doing it right. You gotta make it exactly how the ingredients were initially pitched to the person, and how it's supposed to taste, and how it's supposed to look, and how it's supposed to feel. And that's the problem when you start rushing and cutting corners. In life you end up old with the gout in your foot, five failed marriages, a stripper daughter, and a no-good son. You are the human equivalent of a crooked ass, pickleless 99-cent Big Mac. Sometimes the simplest shit makes the most sense.

SNITCHING

A good friend takes the rap for your ass. If some bullshit is going down, he's in the yard, making sure you're protected. I mean, that's what real friends do, but now I'm gonna be honest: If some shit goes down and you didn't do it, you better snitch on someone; and if there's no one around but that good ass friend, your best bet is to snitch on that muthafucka. There is an expression that goes "Snitches get stitches." Now, I don't know if that's true, but what I do know is that muthafuckas who wind up in jail get stitches, mostly to sew up their stretched-out assholes.

That being said, I'm not advocating snitching—snitching is a bad look. What I'm telling you to do is to not snitch directly. Here's what you do: You snitch to the other snitches. You see, you have to fragment the snitch. You find yourself a blabbermouth (there are plenty out there). That way you are indirectly attached to the snitch, and you still did your duty.

Make sure you are discreet about your snitch. Don't make it seem like you're snitching; just encourage the blabbermouth to move the information forward. Some helpful phrases to use:

"You ain't gonna believe this!"
"I hope nobody calls the cops on his ass, but if they did it, well . . . ☹."
"Between you and me . . ."

Then just sit back and let the authorities handle the rest. And if somehow it comes back to you, just snitch on the blabbermouth you snitched to. See, that shit is symmetry.

POSITIVE SNITCHING

𝔍 tell you, snitching has gotten a bad reputation. To snitch just means to inform on someone; it doesn't say anything about sending someone to jail. What I'm trying to say is that just like you can snitch negative stuff, you can also snitch positive stuff. That's why, if I was technologically inclined, I would make a mint with this idea—and don't steal this shit—*the Positive Snitch App.* This app would send texts, emails, and phone calls to your significant other to positively snitch on you. The messages start off like they are going to be scandalous, but they end up positive.

Let's say you're cheating on your girlfriend and you fuck around and leave your jacket at her place—and the jacket your lady gave you is an anniversary gift. Open up the app, punch in the details, and then before your ass gets whupped, your lady will get this text:

> You don't know me, but I was in the supermarket and I saw
> your man—I think you were on the phone with him—anyway,
> I had this tight skirt on and I bent over and it ripped! Girl, you
> know what your man did? He took off his jacket and handed it
> to me to wrap around my big booty. When he did, he dropped

his phone, and I saw your name and number with a heart
emoji, so I memorized the number to text you to tell you what a
good ass man you've got!

Pretty good, huh? I added the "big booty" part to make it more realistic, because your lady knows you and she knows you wouldn't be so ready to help some lady unless she had a big booty. Now, when you walk in the door, before you can even begin to lie about the jacket, she's like, "Baby, I know what happened. You are such a gentleman! Come here!" See that! I've got a lot of *get your ass out of trouble* ideas. Billionaires, hit me up, I'm always looking for investors.

SELF-ESTEEM DEFENSE

People take up martial arts as self-defense. That's misguided advertising. Don't spend your money learning how to lift your leg up so high you can kick the side of someone's face, 'cause that won't defend you. Let me tell you something, if you threw a kick at me, I would grab your damn fake ass karate leg, twist you to the fuckin ground, and embarrass you! Don't try that shit on me! And definitely don't try it on some desperate ass criminal. Look, I know you're going to want to, I mean, you've been training for a bunch of years, mastering your skill, waiting for the opportunity to try your shit out. I mean you can't practice that shit on your family what you gonna do, chop your grandparents in the throat while they're napping, leg sweep your nephew? You need some bully to come fuck with you so you can look him in the eye and say, "You picked the wrong one!" And then that day finally comes, and someone calls you out and you square up, ready to do your shit, only he doesn't throw a punch, he just looks at you and laughs, he makes fun of your dumbass karate stance and your little ass head and your big ass feet. Then he starts riding your lady's hairstyle. Damn! So now you gotta do something, you get so mad you lift your leg up to bring the muthafuckin' Ruckus with a roundhouse for his ass, he catches your shit like I would. And in the three seconds it took to do a move that should've only taken one, you realize you can't bring the Ruckus to someone if you don't have it in you to begin with. And as he is punching you in the face repeatedly, you realize the classes were bullshit and so were you, and really the reason you bought that martial arts Groupon three years ago wasn't because you wanted to learn about karate, it was 'cause you wanted to gain discipline and learn about yourself.

Deep shit huh? Seriously you want self-defense? You've got to work on self, I call it *Self-Esteem Defense.* One thing I know for a fact is no one can beat me at a mind game! My Ruckus game is tight. You can't shake me in a fucking mind game! I may not look it but trust me one thing I got is a warehouse full of unopen boxes of self-esteem! They say the best offense is a good defense but they got that shit backwards! Protect yourself by strengthening your mind!

Now I'm not saying don't learn how to physically protect yourself but as you've read so far there are better ways to get in that brain ass. For instance, shut the fuck up once in a while and just watch people. Doing this will help you develop your *wenta* muscle, which is important for survival. Trust me, knowing *wenta* talk shit and *wenta* shut the fuck up just might save you from embarrassment.

A good way to enter the mental state necessary to master your mind is to achieve Zen. Now while I recommend practicing it, just be aware of where and when you are doing it. I mean, don't do it while operating heavy machinery or filling out important paperwork and definitely don't try it in the middle of a fight. I highly suggest doing it while sitting on the toilet, preferably in a guest or basement bathroom or rarely used powder room where you are least likely to have someone pounding on the door and ruining your concentration. Sitting on the toilet is a great time to focus on your mind, your body, and your shit. Bottom line: Once you get your brain right you will be able to mind-slap the shit out of a muthafucka right, to the side of the head, and trust me he won't be able to catch it.

SHUTTING SHIT DOWN

One thing I know about being in a relationship is that arguments happen. And at the core of most arguments is dis-re-fuckin-spect! The majority of the time, disrespect occurs when you speak the truth to your partner but you do it in the wrong way! Bottom line: If you have some shit to say that's bothering you, it's better to keep that shit to yourself. But if you find you must say something, here's a suggestion: Start your statement with "No disrespect." Once you say "No disrespect," it gives you the freedom to disrespect. Also, you might try adding "Honestly" or "I'm just saying." Shit like that technically puts you in the clear, because I mean, you've clearly stated that you don't mean to disrespect and you're only being honest.

Despite my great advice to you, as I mentioned before, if you speak your mind to your partner, an argument will follow. Now, in general, I feel the best way to end an argument is to punch the person you are arguing with in the fucking face. That usually just stops the whole argument instantly. But if you're fighting with a woman, never—I repeat, *never*—lay hands on a woman; I don't play that shit. Now, that is not to say that I have never felt like it and I'm sure a lady or two has felt like doing the same to

me, but I can't say it enough: not only should you not touch your lady like
that, she shouldn't touch you like that either; it should never come down
to some shit like that. No, instead, you and your wife should always have
a wide selection of premade pies in the fridge, 'cause trust me, a pie to the
face is the way to go—in particular, pies in the cream and meringue family. Nothing heavy, like pumpkin or like a cobbler; shit like that will do
damage. No, you make sure you use something like a coconut custard or,
better yet, a banana cream. (Make sure it's a flavor you both like, in case
makeup sex occurs—that way you can enjoy licking it off each other.) See?
Now when the police show up on account of a "domestic disturbance"
and the officer sees both of you with pie filling on your faces, that cop is
gonna smirk. I mean, there's no way he can take that shit seriously. Also,
to help your cause, rent a clown suit. If a cop shows up and sees the two of
you standing there dressed like clowns, that cop will have no choice but to
turn his body cam off, get back into that damn patrol car, and drive the
fuck away.

IN IT TO WIN IT

ow, while I believe lotteries are for suckers, I also believe that it is important to play them once in a while. Think about it: No matter how poor you are, no matter how many bills you've run up or how many kids you have when you buy that ticket, right up to the moment you scratch it or that shit draws, you have the possibility of hitting it rich and flying the fuck out of that hole that you're in! A dollar and a fucking dream!

Make sure you enjoy the process; if you don't, then you are probably a degenerate gambler and I'm not speaking to you right now except to say, "Get some damn help!" When you pick numbers, don't do it on the day of the drawing; do it a few days ahead, so you have more time to fantasize. And don't read the winning numbers online or (if you're old) in the papers the next day. You make sure you're in your home and watching that damn drawing wearing a suit or a fancy gown like you're at some damn awards show—that way if you win, you can feel special! Even if you lose, you can pretend you're like Matt Damon or some shit and act like there's a camera in your face and practice your gracious loser face.

Scratch-offs are different. When you buy a scratch-off, make sure to scratch that shit off right there. Don't take it home. And buy at least five at a time to increase your odds! And when you lose, say, "Fuck me!" and walk out the store; let people feel your frustration. Try to avoid this wicked loop: You scratch off and win a free ticket, but then of course you scratch that off and lose, and there you are again screaming, "Fuck me!"

By the way, a lot of people think giving lottery tickets as gifts is a good idea. Well, it might be—right up to the point where your friend wins $1.2 million on that ticket but won't give you shit! That's why you never give lottery tickets as a gift without saying, "Look what I got us!" That way, if they win, legally, "*We* won." You gotta lock down that full "we" coverage. That's fucking important!

INVENTIONS
AND IDEAS

TECHNOLOGY SPEAKING

The show *Silicon Valley* is the shit. I love watching those ugly white kids coding and creating platforms and shit. They're like me: They take the words that you use in one way and twist them up for their own purposes. Like the word "pivot," which is really a dance move, but in tech talk it means changing your ideas or your direction; and "disrupt," which really means ejackalit, but to these cats it just means to cause a ruckus.

If I were going to take over a company in Silicon Valley, I'd take over Apple. They look like they're having fun over there. I mean, all their products have a fucking piece of fruit on them. Everything is white and stylish, but if I were the head of Apple, I would shake things up. Technology is way the fuck behind. It hasn't fixed the old problems, just created random new shit that will create new problems.

Not everybody needs a goddamn laptop or a tiny little Walkman the size of an Altoid where nobody can tell that you're listening to music. What's the fun in that? You need to share the party. I'd bring the boom box back. And I'd make them bigger. I'd still keep the apple on them, because fruit is always welcome, but I'd design some straps so you can walk around with the device on your back. I'm too old to be carrying heavy shit on one shoulder. That shit makes me lopsided, throws my whole body off, and then my dick doesn't know where to go when it's excited. Instead of looking up, it might point to my right foot, and that makes a certain position complicated, if not impossible.

I'd also come up with the idea for a something I would call the double-talk phone. Imagine you were on one phone call with two different ladies but they didn't know the other was on the call! Do you know how useful that would be! Being able to say the same shit once to two different ladies!?! At the same damn time!?! Killing two birds with one damn stone! So if you're setting up a late-night rendezvous, you immediately have given yourself multiple options. Worst-case scenario, if one lady flakes you have a spare; best-case, you wind up with a three-way on a muthafuckin' one-way! Letcha man do this! One pickup line, multiple options—that's fucking technology!

UBERSTAND

ou Uber? What the fuck are you thinking?? You driving for Lyft? What the fuck are you thinking? Weren't ya'll taught to never pick up strangers or get in a car with strangers? But now, all of a sudden, off of reviews from possible psychopaths and a tiny ass picture, y'all go for a ride together, with the hope that you have a mutual Uberstanding that neither one of you will murder the other. But Uberstandings don't mean shit.

Imagine you get picked up one night by a guy named Dou-Dou. Think that doesn't even sound right? Sounds like some made-up shit to you?! Trust me, I've heard some stories! BUT because Dou-Dou has a 3.2 rating and it's late and you're tired, you decide to trust him. You get into his banged-up UberX Corolla that smells like old hot dog water and shame. And then Dou-Dou starts fighting with his wife on the phone in French. He yells at her about his sister-in-law's husband not wanting to be an Uber driver because he's lazy, and really that muthafucka just doesn't want to work at all. All of a sudden Dou-Dou gets so angry that he bangs the dashboard, misses a stop sign, and knocks over an old man on his motorized wheelchair. It's at that point you begin to realize how Dou-Dou lost those rating points, Dou-Dou clearly has some anger issues. Bottom line: while I like and use Uber, never forget you don't know that fucking driver. And every time you hop in one of those bitches, you are violating one of the first things you were taught as a child, right after "Don't go swimming after you eat" and "Don't stand under a tree during a lightning storm," which is "Never take a ride from a stranger!" Uberstand?

UBERFEET

I'm a big walker. I walk all the fucking time, because I like to see shit! (I'm not big on the name-brand sneakers. I just want shoes that fit my fucking feet.) But the walking directions on the map apps could use some improvement.

First off, they need to let you know what's on your route, just like they do with traffic, like "Police reported ahead" or "Car on shoulder." The voice should be telling me, "Dog shit on your right," "Annoying sign spinner in 200 feet." That way you can choose the route that's right for you and also walk with your head up high, knowing the app has got your back.

They also need a walk-sharing app. We could all use someone to come and walk with us. I'd call it Uberfeet. You order someone to come walk with you so you feel safe, and you have someone to bounce shit off of.

Personally, I would be a great person to Uberfeet with. But if you order me, you gotta be patient, 'cause I gotta walk to you from wherever the fuck I am, and maybe that's far away. Or if I'm close, I may have decided to stop by a friend's place to nap or some shit. You could opt for someone closer, but my advice is you might as well wait for me, 'cause you never know who you're gonna get. I would expand this service to other areas, like Ubercoach, where I come over to help you break up with your boyfriend or girlfriend or help throw all their shit out. I thought about Ubermove but I have a bad back. Or Ubercuddle . . . clothing optional.

STRIP PAY

All strippers should have a QR code bracelet, which your cell phone can read and instantly issue payment. And don't tell me that's degrading! Raining filthy money on a stripper is degrading! Do you have any idea where most money has been? If you don't, I'll tell you who does: a stripper. Because it's been up her ass, thanks to stupid ass patrons who are adamant about sticking their singles in her G-string but can't get her to stop shaking, so it winds up in her privates.

I told my man Oscar, he owns a chain of strip clubs that offers a fantastic legs 'n' eggs brunch special. I brought him onboard, and he made a commitment to me that until he gets the QR system installed, he's gonna build a currency exchange station at the entrance. Here patrons would be able to trade in their dirty singles for new, fresh, sanitary bills, for the benefit of every fucking one involved.

I thought it was a pretty good idea until it hit me: Clean money is sticky. People are gonna wanna lick their fingers to separate the bills, and that shit is even worse. That's not gonna help the strippers—it's just opening them up to germs all over again.

See that—sometimes you try to fix shit and wind up making shit worse. Just like that stripper at the club you wanna bring home and make your lady. You hook up with her and you spend all your time trying to get her to stop stripping and make an honest woman out of her but all that does is cause arguments. Man, leave that lady alone, let her do what she wants to do! You don't own her! Then one day you come home from work and find your seventy-inch flat screen and her gone. Some shit just can't be fixed, especially if it ain't broke in the first place.

EDIBLE UNDERWEAR 2.0

I don't know when I first saw some, but I do remember being on the fence about them the first time I did. I'm talking about edible underwear. Better yet, for the rest of this section, so that I don't make myself sick, I will be referring to them as "edible panties." See, when I think of underwear, I think of some crusty old shit-stained drawers, so the idea of something like that being edible is just plain horrible.

Since they first came out, edible panties have always been made out of gummy bear material. While I'm not a big fan of gummy candy, I understand why they were the first choice for them panties. Gummies are stretchy and durable and waterproof—perfect for some panties. But now what if you're someone who can't have sugar but you're getting it on with a lady and she wants you to eat her drawers? Are you gonna push them panties away? Hell no! So there you are, chewing away on those drawers, and the next thing you know you're waking up in a hospital four months later 'cause you're just coming out of a sugar coma! You don't need that kind of shit!

I think they are leaving a lot of money on the table by not making all sorts of other types of edible panties. You need vegetarian ones, sugar-free ones—you need to make them accessible to everyone. And I would stay away from candy-based drawers, especially chocolate-based candies like Milk Duds. In the summer something like that would only cause confusion, not to mention a damn mess! I'm thinking of a more food-based panty, something you would purchase in the food section at the supermarket. And go international with it: If you're about to have sex with a Jamaican, why not get some jerked chicken drawers? Or better yet, make a meal out of it for you and your lady. For instance, you get a pair of ladies' panties made out of pita bread, then you get your men's chorizo underwear. Once you get into bed, you take yours off and she takes hers off, then put your chorizo into her pita. See? The two of you are about to multitask, lunching while fucking!

CRUISES—NOT THE KID

Besides having to roam around Disneyland, Mickey and Minnie gotta spend time on cruise ships too. Any other time you see mice on a fucking boat, that's a fucking sanitation issue, and I believe the same goes here. I don't give a shit that Mickey's got a top coat on like he's in a fucking orchestra conducting.

White people love cruise ships. They get all-inclusive shit so they can eat like piggies, fuck around in the galley in the middle of the night, go into the captain's room, then go back to the fucking buffet with their soft-shell crab and tiramisu.

For black people, however, ships have rough connotations. So I'd make cruise ships designed to address these issues. The white people would be working the ship while us black people would start at the bottom of the ship and have to fight our way up. We would have weapons (like rubber bullets and shit) and we would pretend to kill everybody and get to the top and yell "FREEDOM!!!" 'Cause that's a fucking cruise!

By the time we pulled into the port in the Bahamas, we would get out of our raggedy ass clothes and put our nice shit on. And then we would enjoy the soft-shell crab and tiramisu buffet as free people.

(NOTE: The buffet and weaponry are provided only in the all-inclusive package. If you have the cheaper package, you stay chained the fuck up around your ankles and then we see how you do.)

As free people, we can all enjoy the amenities the cruise ship has to offer, and the cruise ships have fucking everything: post office, babysitting service, screening room, pool. It's better than most neighborhoods. They even have a casino in there.

Beware of the casino. You already spent money on the cruise, now you're just gonna lose your money in the casino. By the time you get to the Bahamas you have no money left, so you gotta just stay in your room. That's fucked up.

On my cruises, you'd be able to wager your room on the cruise ship too. Just like people gamble their house away. And if you lost it at the roulette table or baccarat, you'd just have to walk around for seven days and sit on the lido deck on a lounge chair or something. As a rule, people should be able to gamble anything away. They should be able to take their clothes off, dump them on the roulette table, and see what happens. There should be a surgeon on-site so people can gamble their internal organs as well. So after the game, when the players are forced to walk around the casino naked, with no kidneys or liver, people will know they lost EVERYTHING.

That's some powerful shit.

HEALTH
AND
DIET

TIME TO GET ILL

𝕴'm a pretty damn healthy person. Growing up, the only childhood illness I ever had was the chicken pox. I was pretty damn lucky; kids get a lot of nasty, annoying shit. To be honest, your average kid stays sick, and I blame schools for that. Schools are a breeding ground for all sorts of nasty ass kid afflictions. Besides the big ones, like chicken pox, measles, and the mumps, there's smaller nastier stuff, like pinkeye, head lice, and ringworm. Not to mention all the snot-based, runny-nose illnesses kids get. It's a wonder any of them ever become adults.

I once knew a kid who had the Big Three (chicken pox, measles, and mumps) all at once. Can you imagine that? I don't know if this is true, but I even heard that he also was constipated and had diarrhea at the same damn time! I'm telling you, all anyone could do was talk about that muthafucka: the students, the teachers, the damn principal—his ass was legendary! He missed the whole seventh grade, and they just let his itchy, scabby ass slide right to the eighth. I don't know if that was legal, but I do know it was the right thing to do! Having the Big Three was like a badge of honor! For all the respect he got, that kid might as well have served in Desert Storm!

Luckily, certain illnesses like the ones I mentioned you only get once when you are young—you get them over with nice and early. That's why they call them "childhood diseases." You're a little kid, you ain't got no bills to pay, you're in a position to lie in that bed for a few months with no worries. Your meals will be provided for, someone will rub calamine lotion and help you wash your ass—yes, all is good! Try getting one of those illnesses when you're grown! Try calling out sick from work 'cause your nasty ass has ringworm. See what kind of sympathy you get when you have to walk into the break room with bumps all over your fucking body because you don't have any sick time left. And don't be calling in with a childhood affliction if you're single! How are you gonna explain why you have head lice with no fucking kids around?!

BIGGEST LOSER

ook, what I'm about to say might not be for everybody. I know a lot of people like to diet, but I'm here to tell you diets ain't shit! I have never in my life tried to diet; I love food too damn much! Do you realize how many delicious ass foods there are out there? Take breakfast food for example . . . I love me some damn breakfast! I know a lot of people do, but I'm just saying, I have no problem eating breakfast for dinner—on the other hand, there is also nothing wrong with eating dinner for breakfast. Do you know how many times Larry has caught me in the morning eating his stupid ass dinner-party leftovers—gourmet shit, you know what I mean!?!—shit with truffles in it, or some dish with nasty ass goat cheese, for breakfast!?! See, my appetite is not guided by some damn clock! I don't even wear a watch! Although if I did wear one maybe I would eat when I was supposed to. Maybe that's my secret. Anyway, shit like pancakes, I will eat those tasty muthafuckas anytime of the day! And the great thing about them is that you can customize them to your individual taste. Like blueberries? Throw some in. Like chocolate chips? Throw some the fuck in! Shit, have high blood pressure? Throw in your medication! Oh yeah, say you have a little, sick, stubborn ass kid who came home with a runny ass nose . . . pour some Children's Robitussin or some shit like that in that pancake batter, then toss some bananas or something like that in there to make it look festive. Trust me, that kid will eat and enjoy the fuck out of them damn pancakes and then an hour later be knocked out and wake up later feeling better! And on top of all of that, pancakes have more than one name; I mean, you can also call them "flapjacks" and "hotcakes." Why give one dish three names? How the fuck should I know? Why would I know some shit like that? What I do know is I enjoy each one of them like they are some separate type shit.

Now, I'm not suggesting you eat like me; you see, I have always had a high metabolism! Before you get mad and hate on my skinny ass, just know that a high metabolism is a blessing and a curse; they don't tell you that shit. On the plus side it allows me to eat what the fuck I want, when I want. Oh yeah I can fuck up a few packs of Twinkies at the drop of a dime, I can eat a gallon of ice cream with my eyes closed; no seriously, I have fallen asleep in a tub of ice cream many times. Man, I can eat one eight-course meal, two four-course meals, or eight one-course meals and not think anything of it! But by far my favorite thing to eat is Pop-Tarts in the middle of the night. What flavor, you ask? All of them, muthafuckas, all the fruit ones, the fancy ones with designs, the frosted ones! Damn, I love the frosted ones—I'm surprised they haven't made a frosted-filled frosted one!

All that being said, I do realize that most of you don't have a metabolism like mine. For muthafuckas like you I'm about to give you a word that I'm pretty damn sure I know the meaning of . . . "moderation"! You easy-gaining-weight muthafuckas just need to learn that you *can* have all the shit you want, but unlike me, not as much as you want and not when you want it. For example, if you like cheesecake, eat all the cheesecake you want, just make sure you eat it in a steam room. That cheesecake experience will wind up being so damn awful for you that you will probably never want cheesecake again. And as for the calories, you might not lose weight but you probably won't gain any, either. Look, you just have to know you. Be fair to yourself but be real with yourself. When a friend with body issues asks, "Do I look fat?" of course you say "no"—that's a responsible lie. But if you ask yourself that, and you are, don't lie to yourself. I mean, why the fuck would you lie to you? If you can't trust you who can you trust? And even if you have an answer for that question can you trust it considering the fact that you can't trust you? See what I mean!?!

PART-TIME VEGETARIAN/
FULL-TIME CANNIBAL

These days people are all about labels to define who they are. Why do that? Why try to define yourself? Why limit yourself! I mean, people even label what kind of eater they are. I'll tell you what kind of eater I am: whatever the fuck *she* is! That's 'cause women tend to care about shit like that more than men. You tell a vegetarian woman that you eat meat, and it's a wrap. By the way, have you ever eaten a wrap? How about a wrap inside of another wrap? That shit is fucked up. You go home, the lights are off 'cause you didn't pay your bill or some shit, and you're hungry and you eat the wrap, but you're not sure if you unwrapped the right wrap, so you end up eating half the paper wrap. I didn't realize it until I had eaten half the damn thing. Where was I? Oh yeah, whatever she eats, I eat. I don't give a fuck what it is!

That isn't to say I don't have a preference. If it was left up to me, I would eat only sexy foods, shit like spaghetti. I love me some damn spaghetti! And believe me, when you're with a lady and you want to be sexy, you make her some Italian food. Remember the great scene in *Lady and the Tramp* when the two dogs are sucking down spaghetti and it turns out they're sucking the same strand? That moment blew my mind, it gave me a hard-on! Don't judge me: Cartoon spaghetti is the best!

People ask me if I cook. Of course I do, but I cook for survival. I don't do stupid ass dinner parties, I cook single-serve shit. I'll count sixteen fucking spaghettis if I know that's all I need to eat, and that's all I make. I also make ketchup from scratch, 'cause that's fucking impressive. Paul Newman made salad dressings and really good movies, but he didn't make ketchup. Big mistake.

Also, I make a hell of a pot pie! Pot pies are old school shit, like stew and casseroles. Pot pies are amazing and so easy to make. You can put whatever you want in there: vegetables, rice, anything. Shit, if you're making it for a children's party, you could put candy and toys in there like a piñata. The key is simply this: If you're making a chicken pot pie, just make sure you have more chicken in there than any other ingredient. Pretty simple. I mean, if you fuck around and have more rice in there, then you'll be stuck with a rice pot pie, and trust me, nobody wants that shit.

And here's a tip: A pot pie a day keeps the doctor away. People say an apple a day does, but an apple is not the meal that a pot pie is. An apple is just a snack. You need a whole damn meal to keep a doctor away. Not to mention, a pot pie is way more practical than a fucking apple. You can't freeze an apple, then put it in the fucking microwave three months later. If you tried it once you defrosted that apple, it would come out brown and look terrible, and most likely if you put that shit in the microwave it would just explode.

Here's another expression for you: "You are what you eat." People say that dumb shit all the time. Problem is, the only people it's true for, when you think about it, are cannibals. Everyone else just eats food. Now, I know I could never be a cannibal, but I tell you, if I was forced to be one, I would be a vegetarian cannibal. The way I see it, I grew up eating a shit-load of meat. My family loves meat. When I was a kid, I didn't ask for no ice cream for dessert, I asked for a meat dessert. I would cry for some bear pudding or a mutton pancake. In our house, we ate all kinds of wild game, wild ass turkey, rabbits and shit. Vegans find that shit hard to swallow. They don't eat anything that blinks or cries. I forget. That way of life doesn't leave much to survive on, so to get their vitamin intake, they eat super healthy.

If I were a cannibal, I would be a vegetarian cannibal: That is to say that I would only eat vegetarians. I mean, if you're gonna eat someone, you want to at least make sure you're eating someone who is healthy. If you eat someone, you're eating everything they've eaten. Every last bit of food, every damn Twinkie—you eat him, you're eating all that shit! If they've got high cholesterol and you eat them, guess what: *You've* got high cholesterol. Plus, just by eating a vegetarian, I'd be getting the meat and the vegetable all at once: a perfectly balanced meal.

STAYING HEALTHY

SPOT ME

Most people go to the gym and build up the wrong parts of their bodies. I work on something called the "Get the Fuck Off Me" muscles. People worry about being offensive, like those karate mutha-fuckas. All the time learning shit they won't use. Those cats just have to stand around waiting for somebody to touch them so they can fuck them up. That's some useless bullshit.

Y'all are wasting your time with useless workouts. We are not training for the goddamn Olympics. Nobody's gonna survive walking up a fuck-ing StairMaster or using a fucking rowing machine. My workout emulates real-life situations. It gives you skills to survive. You follow the workout guidelines and do your fucking exercises the right way, you won't be able to enter a baseball stadium without the entire crowd whispering, "Damn, that man is bringing the ruckus. Don't fuck with him."

With my workout, you have to enter the gym or your homemade workout area with the look of a killer. You have to clench your teeth and keep repeating the mantra "Get the fuck off me, get the fuck off me."

Now, if you're alone during your workout, you'll have a harder time getting the desired benefits. It's like doing a self-defense class where you're attacking yourself. Kinda hard to kick yourself in the balls.

So take a buddy with you. Someone you respect but also want to fuck up. This person will personify various villains, innocent bystanders, and law enforcement who you may encounter on the street.

Some of these exercises are modifications of existing ones already in the field.

Like the Bench Press. You get your buddy to spot you, so when you're pushing up, they're pushing that shit down, while they're talking shit about you to your face. Like really nasty shit that brings up childhood memories and shit. (To prep for that, you gotta take stock. Sit down at your stupid ass IKEA desk and make a list of all the shit you hate about yourself, everything you're insecure about, every abusive word your mother or father threw at you growing up.) Your buddy hurls all this shit at you, getting you angrier and angrier, motivating you to push harder and harder against his resistance.

Now, if you're an emotional muthafucka, this bench press can get dangerous, 'cause instead of getting angrier and pushing harder, you're just gonna break down and cry like a baby. So if you know yourself to be sensitive and kind of a pussy, make sure the insults you put together are not too personal. Maybe they revolve around rough shit in the world, like global warming and starving kids and disappearing rain forests.

FLU DICK

When it comes to illnesses, there are lots of medicines and treatments to deal with them, but, see, I'm more about prevention. So with that being said, I want to take a moment and talk to you about a preventable affliction that many men walk around with every damn day.

I'm talking about Flu Dick. Fortunately it is preventable, and I am here to bring awareness to this highly transmittable virus.

Dudes. You walk around all day touching random shit: doorknobs, subway poles, money. Worse yet, you touch nastier shit—other muthafuckas! You walk around high-fiving, fist bumping, and handshaking muthafuckas, thus allowing for the potential of contracting the virus. I myself avoid casual physical contact with other muthafuckas, but if you're in a situation where you absolutely must touch someone to greet them—I'm talking like a prince or a governor, a former president, or like a maharishi or some shit—I suggest giving a pound or a fist bump. Contrary to popular belief, you are much less likely to contract a virus with a pound or a fist bump versus a handshake or a high five. You might notice that I have distinguished between the fist bump and the pound. Pounds are for the average person, they are easy to pull off; when someone sees you getting ready to give their ass a pound, they are in turn ready to give one back.

But a fist bump is not always as easy to read, and what can happen is you could be going in for a fist bump while that other muthafucka is going in for a handshake and wind up punching that courteous damn man on the hand and breaking his fingertips. That being said, both a fist bump and a pound limit the amount of time you are making contact with that filthy fucking maharishi, and that's important because it's during that crucial moment when you are on the path to either contracting or transmitting Flu Dick. Not to mention muthafuckas who like to give high fives are usually too excited, and that shit gets annoying. This has nothing to do with Flu Dick, I'm just pointing that out.

Now you got the flu on your fucking hands but you don't know it. It's not as though your hands turn blue like when you're robbing a bank and that hatin' ass teller sneaks one of those exploding ink packs in the money bag. That shit's fucked up. It would almost be a good thing if the virus turned your hand blue, that way you'd know who not to fuck with. I said almost, 'cause trust me, that shit is hard to get off. Like I said, you have the virus on your hands, now here's how your dick gets it.

You go to the bathroom. Proper procedure, if you're not a completely filthy muthafucka, is that you wash your hands before leaving the bathroom, but if you want to prevent Flu Dick, you are going to have to be more vigilant than that. You have two choices: either wash your hands before and after, or, better and more effective, wash your hands after and then wash your damn Johnson. Now, I understand some of you might feel uncomfortable washing your Johnson in the sink in front of strangers, but remember you are woke and they're not, so enlighten them. So if you're there drying your Johnson with one of them rough ass paper towels or that hot air blower and somebody says some shit to you, just look his ass in the eye and say, "I'm preventing Flu Dick, muthafucka," and handle your business.

Unfortunately, though, most men don't know the proper cleaning procedure that I mentioned, so back to what I was saying. You go into the bathroom and just take your dick out with your dirty ass flu hands, relieve yourself, and then put your Johnson back in your pants, and boom! You just got flu dick. You go home, you walk into the house, you make love to your wife with your flu dick, and now her pussy, formerly known as healthy, has got the flu. That's fucked up and you know it. The solution is so obvious it pisses me off: wash your hands *before* you pull your dick out. And wash them again when you're done.

Together we can make Flu Dick a thing of the past.

PUSSY TEA

$\mathfrak{I}$f it hasn't been clear to you by now, I love me some pussy! Don't get me wrong, I respect it—but trust me, I will beat it up at the same time!!! I love the look of pussy, the smell of pussy, but especially the taste of pussy. That being said, I don't eat pussy, and if you wanna get technical with it, no one eats pussy. You might lick it, lap it, slurp it, and tap it—but you damn sure don't *eat* pussy. Really, the thought of literally eating pussy is a horrible image. Which kind of makes me wonder where the term came from. Shit, more than that, who was the first person to do it! I bet you the answer to one of those questions is the answer to the other. I'm guessing the first brave soul that decided to get on Route 95 and head south was the muthafucka who coined the phrase. His shocked and excited ass lady probably looked down at him and asked what the fuck he was doing, and in the moment he said, "Eating your damn pussy," and that shit just stuck. I mean, why wouldn't it? You think in the middle of all of that pleasure she was gonna contradict him? Hell no! So "eating pussy" became the name for it! To be honest, he could have looked up and said anything and it would've stuck: "I'm at an all-you-can-eat smorgasbord!" "I'm chewing some pussy gum!" "I'm doing a lap around the pond!" Whatever that brave explorer would have said, it would have stuck.

Now, as much as I love the taste of it, I must admit that I don't like all the shit that goes along with getting it. I mean, we all like going to the carnival: The rides are fun, the food is sweet, and we wind up screaming a bit. That's a lot like a good pussy-tasting experience. But sometimes on the way to the carnival there's traffic, the road is bumpy, and bad smells start coming through your vent. And once you get to the carnival, you find that the rides are old, sticky, smelly, and some are even broken. That's a bad pussy experience.

On top of it, most good pussy comes with some sort of commitment. Think not? Whether written or verbal, trust me, it's there. Now, sometimes you are ready for that commitment. I mean, you found the right one, or you've reached the right moment in your life, or in a few extreme cases someone named you in a will but said you need to be married by a certain age. If any of these scenarios apply to you, congratulations: You are committed to some pussy. For most people, though, that sort of commitment for just a taste is too much! And that's why I've come up with an amazing invention: Pussy Tea!

Go bag some pussy essence and start marketing it as tea, and you will make a fortune. You could sell it in places like 7-Eleven as Pussy Tea, or class it up a bit and sell it in high-end specialty markets as Vagina Tea. Look, at the end of the day, most people don't want sex, they just want the taste of pussy. Or they can't get sex and they still want the taste of pussy. Even women: Most are bi-curious but too afraid to admit it. This way they can dabble without going all in or hurting anybody's feelings or alienating their parents.

I can see the commercial now: some cool ass man sitting at a tea house, stirring his pussy tea with his finger, when all of a sudden a friend comes by and is like, "What's that?" And the dude gently pulls his finger from that cup and says, "Pussy tea. Here, smell my finger!" And then the slogan pops up onscreen: "Pussy Tea: *All of the Taste . . . None of the Commitment*." If there's anyone out there in marketing who wants to get in on this, lemme know—we could be rich!

DRUG YOUSE

$\mathfrak{I}$'m not gonna sit here and advocate drugs, but I'm also not gonna sit here and say I don't understand why some people do them. If you're gonna do drugs, don't be doing some hard core bullshit like coke or meth, or especially heroin. Heroin is a drug where you've got to get on another drug to get off of it! That's like having your foot on the gas and the brakes all at one time.

Nah, stick to peaceful shit, the shit that gives you something like an out-of-body experience. Like a pot brownie. "Out of body" means your soul separates from your physical body like the egg and the yolk when the chef cracks that shit over the bowl. Your egg white separates from the yolk and your ass is standing there looking at yourself, sitting on the sofa. You wave to yourself and yourself waves back, you're both feeling it. Shit, the way I see it, while you're outside your body you might as well do stuff your physical self wouldn't do.

Might as well enjoy life a bit more: go hit on that honey you've had your eye on for a while, go tell your boss how you really fucking feel about him or her. You can do all kinds of shit. Take advantage of being outside. Don't forget that your inner self is invisible now, so go sneak into a heavy metal concert, and while you're at the concert walk into the ladies' room. Why not? They can't see you. Live a little!

Most important to remember, though: Don't fuck with another brownie while you're out of your body. Remember, there are a lot of aspects to a person's personality. Fuck around and eat a tray of brownies, and there will be a whole lot of different versions of you floating around—angry you, happy you, single you, married you, out-of-the-closet you . . . a lot of yous. So as the original you is floating around, you will wind up seeing a whole bunch of other yous engaged in a variety of shit. For instance, you might see a cop slam another you on the hood of a patrol car while a third you is standing there posting that shit to Facebook, talking about "Leave him alone, he didn't do anything! All he did was eat a damn brownie!" All off a sudden a crowd of yous pops up out of nowhere chanting "Yous Lives Matter!" And they have Yous Lives Matter t-shirts, only some of them have it as "Y-o-u-s-e" and some have it with "Y-o-u-s." So they all start arguing as to which is correct—yup, all the yous, crazy shit. Meanwhile the original you is trying to point out that both of them are improper grammar, but as that you is being all condescending and shit with it, one of the angry yous gets offended and pops the original you in the head with a brick.

See what I'm talking about? That's why I don't do drugs. Shit can get out of hand quickly! Besides, social movements are too important to fuck around with, you need clarity for that shit.

THE FIVE DEADLY STEPS

$\mathfrak{I}$'m not a drinker, I'm one who likes to be in control at all times. I've faked being drunk before, though, just like for those of you guys out there who have sadly had to experience a woman fake an orgasm. I mean, I can't imagine what that shit must be like, because it could never happen to me. See, when I make love to a lady I make sure to keep a can of silly string between my box spring and my mattress, and if I even sense a fake orgasm coming on, like her heart isn't into it or she's distracted thinking of some food burning on the stove, the goddamn smoke alarm going off, the bath-water overflowing, the fire department chopping a hole in the door (they love chopping shit), or her husband, I counter her fake ass moaning with some louder fake ass moaning, like I'm about to explode. And while she's being razzle-dazzled by my supposed come countdown, I slide my hand between that damn box spring and mattress and discreetly spray that silly string all over the goddamn room, the walls, the ceiling, her, her damn cat. When you turn the lights on in that room, it should look like they had a damn silly string party in that muthafucka. I call that faking da fuck! See, I gets mine, Larry, even when I'm not getting mine.

Now if I can fake some male ejackalit, you know I can fake the fuck out of being drunk. Which is ironic, because drunk people are the most honest people in the world, and they really understand me like nobody else. But if you're going to get fucked up, you have to plan ahead. Start by figuring out what kind of drinker you are:

- **Nice (aka social drinker):** 85 percent of people at a party are this one: nice, charming people willing to approach strangers and engage in annoying small talk. For these drinkers, the booze brings out a better you. More confident. Engaging. The kind I can tolerate. Lady social drinkers make men feel better because they laugh at 60 percent of their stupid jokes that don't deserve even a chuckle. Male social drinkers make women feel better because they're able to pretend they actually care about what comes out of their mouth while they are imagining the ejackalit party at their house later.

- **Tipsy:** These fools trip more and spill shit. They are totally capable of getting home on their own but call for an Uber limo by accident and then blurt out that they "deserve it." Tipsy people tend to wish they were Fucked Up—they are amateurs who think being Fucked Up is a badge of honor. Tipsy people want people to think they have a drinking problem. They will talk about their weekends at work and tell people how Fucked Up they were, but are always reminded that they were only Tipsy. It has to be pointed out to them that if they were really Fucked Up, they wouldn't remember shit.

- **Lit:** These fools get nasty, and they bark at other people about how fake they are. These cats order an Uber just to have people to argue with. Lit drinkers are coherent enough to actually say "I'm fucking Lit" and then be able take their ass to the bathroom before they piss on themselves. Lit people also tend to ask you, "Do I look fucked up?" Being Fucked Up is of great concern to them. To reassure someone who is Lit, ask them if they've thrown up in their mouth yet. If they say no, let them know they are not Fucked Up, they are just Lit.

- **Belligerent:** I don't waste time trying to understand these muthafuckas. They usually wake up the next day missing a fucking shoe.

- **Fucked Up:** These individuals tend to experience unwanted pregnancies. They call a friend to get home and then insist on running errands that they remember from some other time in their life, like returning a prom tux or getting a wisdom tooth removed. Unlike Lit drunks, Fucked Up drunks are not able to make it to the bathroom, nor do they even try to, and thus they are also known as Pissy drunks. And while Lit drunks wish to be Fucked Up, Fucked Up drunks don't actually give a fuck. As a result they quite often wake up next to strangers ranging from hookers to hobos and are usually in possession of a Belligerent's other shoe.

DR. DOCTOR, PhD

Don't waste your money on fucking psychiatrists. All they do is re-peat the shit you're saying, except they add a question mark at the end. And don't think for a second that they don't go home and tell their spouse all your damn business. That's what all couples do when they get home: They share the ridiculous shit that happened during their day, and you told that psychiatrist all your damn secrets. You, my friend, are that ridiculous shit. That damn psychiatrist lies in his bed watching Dr. Phil and giggling his ass off!

All psychiatrists watch Dr. Phil, they love him! They want to be him! And why the fuck not?! He does what they do, except he's rich. Also, while they have the same damn patients coming in each week boring them with the same damn crazy problems, *he* only has to listen to a pa-tient once. He has a guest on, makes fun of the guest a bit, and then gets rid of that muthafucka! And to top it off, he gets to end every show by walking out of the studio with his little ass wife. Every . . . damn . . . show! I'm telling you, I've never seen him walk off without her. Have you? He loves that lady, or maybe he's co-dependent on her. You don't know, do you? See, that's what a good psychiatrist does: He gets you trying to analyze him.

Look, you wanna save some money—let me analyze your ass! I promise you I would get to the bottom of your problems.

Think I don't know how? Whatchu think I do with the man whose house I live in? I listen to his bullshit, stare him dead in his blurry ass eyes, and set him straight. I just don't charge him. Trust me, though, I've been keeping a mental tally and I know how much he owes me. If he ever asks me for rent, I will present his ass with an invoice for mental services rendered. Nothing better to shut a muthafucka up then to present him with an invoice he wasn't expecting for some shit. And I wouldn't just hand it to him, I would put that shit in an envelope, put a stamp on it, and mail it from his house to his house. Then when the mail came and he got that letter from me with the same mail to and return address and came to me to ask what it was, I would be like, "An invoice, muthafucka, now what?! You think this shit free?"

Let me tell you something, if I was a therapist, I wouldn't have a damn office, I would have you meet me at one of those filthy hourly rate hotels, you know the ones? They're for lovers who don't want to get caught making love. And see, those places are, what, like twenty-five, thirty dollars an hour, so already I'm saving you money. So I would get you in there, lay you down on that damn bedbug-riddled mattress, and tell you to relax and ask you for two dollars. Then I would go down the hall to the vending machines and get a bag of Cheese Nips and a can of Mountain Dew and then head back to the room to get to the bottom of your shit. And as you lie there in that scary room, sounds from the dangerous ass neighborhood will come leaking in through the single-pane windows: sirens, car alarms, screams, broken glass. All of a sudden everybody in that damn hotel would start fear fucking! It's like *Fear Factor* but it's Fear Fucking. Which, speaking as a therapist, is the best way to confront fear. Then you hear the sound of someone getting fucked in the room to the left and someone getting fucked up in the room to the right, which, by the way, if both are being done properly, you shouldn't be able to tell the difference. See, that's some deep psychiatrist right there. Anyway, the whole situation will be so damn horrible and you'll want to get out of there so fast that you'll realize your problems aren't so bad after all. Problem fucking solved.

See, you don't need to waste money on a damn psychiatrist, or no specialist for that matter. Wanna know why health care costs so much? Too many goddamn specialists. Doctors should be required to have at least two specialties. Take a psychiatrist and a dentist: One works inside your head and one works outside, but really, they should both be able to get in there. Combine them in one medical professional. And if I had to pick, I'd rather be leaning back in a dentist's chair with him asking me questions about my childhood while he tries to get in my mouth.

Plus, dentists have a spit sink, which is pretty fantastic.

One doctor hybrid that wouldn't work: psychiatrist-gynecologist! Can't work on your head from there. Doesn't work in particular because you might trust a gynecologist while he's fiddling downstairs, asking you how your head is feeling, but you would not like a psychiatrist while he's asking you about your relationship with your father asking a question about your coochie. You don't need the psychiatrist dabbling into your fields.

Really, in the end, you're better off just buying a fucking parrot: They're gonna repeat what you say too, and they won't charge you three hundred dollars an hour. Get a parrot or, better yet, a cockatoo. That's one good-looking bird with one cool ass name. Let me tell you something about those birds: Give that bird a compliment, he'll give it right back to you. Do you know how therapeutic it is to have a pretty bird call you a pretty bird?

FOOD FOR THOUGHT

FLIX AND CHICKS

𝕴 love going to see the movies in the theater. I don't get all you cats who watch movies at home. Spend thousands of dollars on huge ass TVs. All that streaming shit is for losers. This country is fat enough as it is, now people are too fucking lazy to get in their cars to drive to the movie theater. The only reason to watch a flick at home is so that you can rub one out without getting arrested. But why would you want to see anything without a hundred people around you laughing and screaming along with you? That's the communal experience. That's why we were put on this earth.

I like action movies with just a hint of titty. Like Bond films from the 1960s. Bond would get some sexy woman, and just as they were about to make love, the screen would go dark. See, that leaves it to your imagination. That's provocative. I would rather imagine for myself what's going on, 'cause my sexual mind is a lot more creative than what's out there. Shit, don't try to figure me out with some half ass bullshit love scene. If you show me some shit, you're just gonna disappoint me. You don't even know what I'm into! For all you know, I like to roll around in a bathtub filled with baby oil and marbles. Better yet, put a woman in that tub, a couple gallons of melted butter, a Costco bag of marshmallows, and a case of Rice Krispies. Let that all set until that lady is at the center of a big ass Rice Krispies treat. Then I would eat my way through that damn Rice Krispies treat until I get to the damn woman! See, that's freaky shit! Type of shit you make your lady sign a release form and a damn confidentiality agreement over! Bonus: Cleanup is simple. You're already in the damn tub, so just turn the water on, grab a loofah, and scrub off all the excess shit that had not been previously orally removed. Last thing you need is to walk out of the house with a sweaty Rice Krispies remnant on your shoulder and have some asshole put two and two together. Next thing you know, muthafucka knows your tricks and word gets around and you're getting less action.

My first celebrity crush overtook me when I saw the great Diahann Carroll appear as Claudine in that movie *Claudine*. Man, she was a beautiful lady! Fuck that, she's still a beautiful lady! She played a single mom with a shitload of delinquent kids, like six or seven of them. She lived in the projects, was on welfare, and was struggling to raise her bad ass kids. There was something about her that was so strong and beautiful! I was just a little kid at the time, but when I saw her, I was ready to step up and be her man! I would have taken on all those responsibilities! You know how hard that would have been on me to have kids that were older than me?! Trying to help them with their homework? Or spank their ass?!? But I would have taken on the challenge, 'cause that's how fine she was!

Sure, today there are plenty of fine ladies on the silver screen, but these days we know too much of their daily routine, with all the *TMZ* surveillance. We know what they look like first thing in the fucking morning right after they take their shit, or when they're on some drug binge in Mexico. So when I do see one of these women on the big screen, all I see is that scary ass lady that took her garbage out that morning or the pasty ass on the beach in Cabo. I prefer to stick to the old school starlets who always looked glamorous and never took a shit. Ever.

In terms of classics, I am not one with the popular consensus. You know what I'm talking about: fucking *Forrest Gump*. That film pisses me the fuck off. It was the wrong movie to make. They should've made the movie about Jenny. That bitch lived her life! She definitely stripped, and she liked the ladies. Jenny got around. You know she had every sexual disease there was, because she wound up getting a sexual disease that didn't even exist yet. Hell, it might've started with her. Patient Zero or whatever you call that shit. And come on, you know that smart ass kid was not Forrest's. She was fucking some professor at some nearby community college.

One flick that definitely would not have worked: *Bubba*. Bubba was as dumb as Forrest, but you cannot be dumb as Forrest *and* black. In the South! You can't even get a good trailer out of that story—the footage would have burned the movie projector.

And horror movies? These days horror movies are fucking bullshit. It's either special effects or fucking zombies. Zombies just look like strung-out crackheads. I can see those fools anywhere. Why do I gotta pay money to see them chasing white people in groups? Now, *Sunset Boulevard*, that was a fucking horror movie. I would have run that old lady's ass to the ground like a rental car. As scary as she was, that's all she really wanted. And that stupid fuck wouldn't give it to her. If I was there, that movie would have had a lot different ending, with me throwing pool parties and shit, giving her my cell phone to take as many close-ups of herself as she wanted. Everybody would have been fucking happy.

CAT DOG MONKEY
FALCON SOUP

Someone's gotta shake up the dog training. Roll over, play dead. That shit has gotten old. Even the dogs are like, "Enough already with this bullshit. Teach us something cool." I'll tell you what's the shit: teaching dogs how to chew gum. Do you know how cool that would look? Especially if you grabbed a piece too. You'd be walking down the street with your dog, chewing together, keeping rhythm. That's true harmony and connection. Of course, you gotta make sure the dog won't swallow the gum, choke, and die. That would not look as cool. Still working on how that would work.

Regardless, I'd stay away from Chihuahuas. They look way too nervous to be chewing. One piece of gum could send them over the edge. And nobody looks cool with a Chihuahua anyway. They are a ridiculous breed.

A friend of mine got a dog as a gift and didn't want him, so he dropped him off at the park. I was like, "Why did you do that? Why didn't you just take him back to the shelter?" A couple of days later, the dog showed up at his door, and that shit created a whole new dilemma. What do you do with this damn dog? He clearly knows your address! Do you take him to another park farther away? Do you move or maybe just change the numbers on your building to confuse the dog? Poor little fucker standing there and being like, "I could've sworn it was 273. Shit, I must be getting old."

If you're gonna get a cat, get one of those weird ass hairless ones. That way you get the security features a cat offers without any of the hair to clean up. Petting one of those hairless cats is like caressing a really expensive leather purse, and who doesn't love that shit?

Now, if you really want a pet that you can become friends with, go for a monkey. Monkeys are the best. They'll peel your bananas and make you laugh all day. And if you keep one on your shoulder, everybody is gonna want to talk to you and give you money like you're some traveling vaudeville guy or some shit like that. Just make sure they're not rabid so you don't die.

If you don't want other people, money, or conversation, then go for the decadent pet: the falcon. A falcon oozes sophistication and decadence. You gotta get that big ass glove that goes all the way to your shoulder, perch the majestic bird on your hand, and just go walking around like a knight or lord of the fucking manor. That shit is royalty right there.

I have several dogs that go everywhere with me. They're stray dogs that won't go away. A lot of people get dogs for protection. But dogs aren't worth shit in that regard. Sure, they smell and sense fear, but all you gotta do to confuse them is tell them some fucking jokes. That throws them off, and then they won't attack you. For those dogs that don't have a sense of humor, a Milk Bone is enough. I keep a Milk Bone in my pocket at all times, just in case my humor doesn't land with the particular breed I'm trying to avoid.

Point is, if you want to protect yourself and your loved ones, get a cat. Criminals come into your house, it's dark, they hear a cat, they get fucking scared because they know that cat will pounce and scratch their face off. They don't go for Milk Bones and shit. They have expensive tastes, and carrying around a Fancy Feast in your pocket with the can opener is not fucking practical.

SPERM BANK ACCOUNT

From when you're little, you're always taught to put your valuables in a bank. Whether that bank is a big building filled with rich people, cheap lollipops, and a vault or it's a big mayonnaise jar, it is driven into your head that you need to save. Well, I got two damn problems with that. One, if you put all your shit in one place, it's pretty damn easy for all of your shit to turn up missing—like how my jar did one day, coincidentally the same day my daddy got a bad ass new hat. Looking back, he did have a funeral to go to and he did wear that hat and he did eventually leave me that hat, so I guess you could call my jar an investment, something like a 401k with a hat option. Still, when it came down to it, I had a date lined up with this pretty little girl from my English class, and I ain't had a dime to take her out. I was so embarrassed that I stopped going to that English class, which might explain why to this day I say "I ain't got a dime" instead of "I didn't have a dime." See how shit works out?

That's what happens with having your money all in one place. You see it every day: Some rich ass actor goes on a talk show and says he's broke because his accountant or lawyer or business manager or some shit stole all his money. See, I will never have that problem. First of all, I would never trust any of those muthafuckas with my shit! To this day, if you want to hold something of mine, you'll have to let me hold something of yours. Want to borrow five hundred bucks to buy your newborn baby a crib? Sure, just lemme hold your brand-new baby till you pay me back. I bet you I'll get my money back.

Thankfully for me, I don't have money—not because I can't get it, but because it's much easier to not have it. That way I don't have to carry money around or find a place to keep it or hide it. Plus, hiding money is dangerous, because one day you could be at a baseball game and have a foul ball hit you on the head and wind up with one of them tall lumps and amnesia. Ever find a bag of money? How do you think it got there? Someone with amnesia left it there. Damn shame!

All of this brings me to the only bank I use, and that's a sperm bank, because to be quite honest, the only thing of value that I ever carry around with me is my sperm. And trust me, it's very valuable! Now, not only do I go to sperm banks, I *enjoy* going! Hell, I make a weekend of it! Oh yeah, I get in one of those nice comfy rooms and I make myself at home! Wanna know how? First of all, most of those places offer you some porn to help you along with the process. But trust me, their stuff is bullshit: a lot of women with flat asses fuckin' in the missionary position. Like I said, bullshit! Here's what you do: You show up in a robe and some boxers, carrying your own pillow, blanket, and your own damn porn, hard core shit!!! Come in there carrying DVDs with donkeys, catapults, and all sorts of shit on the cover—and make sure it's all visible! Tell the person at the front desk you'll need a room for two, and when she looks at you sideways, tell her that *you* are the two! Hell, you're gonna be making love to yourself. I mean, that's what you're doing, so own that shit! And if she's good-looking, tell her if she's not busy later, you and yourself might be looking for a third! Once your provocative entrance is done, take your shit and head into your room.

Once you're in that room, don't feel rushed. Remember, that door locks from the inside. Plus, they are not gonna come knocking at that door for a while, and even when they do, it will be a gentle tap on the door and a soft "How are you doing in there?" So pace yourself, relax, eat a snack, watch a game on your phone, or just chill. During the course of your masturbatory weekend, after that first tap at the door, if you hear someone approaching the door again, start making a lot of loud sex noises. A loud, passionate "Oh shit!" will most definitely cause any nurse or orderly to jump back and go about their business. After the first day, you might have to make an appearance to let them know you didn't ejackalit yourself to death. What you do is you splash some water on yourself to look like you've worked up a sweat and then come out with no drawers on and your robe wide open. Step up to that front desk, look that damn front-desk lady in the face, and give her a nice, loud, sexually satisfied, "WOOOOOO! Round Two!!!" Then ask that lady for some water or, better yet, juice. When she brings it to you, no matter how big the container, you chug that shit completely! And be sloppy with it: Let it run out of your mouth and drip all down your chest and shit! See, that gives off the idea that you are insatiable! Nothing can satisfy your thirst, so in turn, nothing will stop you from trying to quench that damn thirst! Trust me, either she follows you back to the room or everyone will stay the fuck away from you and leave you alone. Either way, you get a weekend stay.

One last thought on sperm banks: They need to run them like weed dispensaries. From what I have been told, weed dispensaries name the different strains of weed that they offer—that way you know what you're getting. For instance, you hear some name like Dolly Parton, you know the weed will make your chest feel heavy. Sperm banks need to name their various sperm offerings—that way people who come there to make a withdrawal know what the fuck they're getting. Want to know what I would call mine? I'll tell you. Now, although I'm not religious, it would seem to me that having a baby using a sperm bank is kind of an alternative route—I mean, you're actually missing out on the best part of having a baby, and that is making that muthafucka. But considering I once read about a famous baby that was supposed to have been born without the act of some parental fucking, and since I would not have the pleasure of fucking whoever had selected my fine sperm, I came up with this name: Immaculate Ejackalit! Don't try to steal it, I have a copyright pending.

CATFISH AND GRITS

I hear all this talk about Catfish and Catfishing, and all of it is bad. Look, if someone tricks your ass, that's on you. I mean, you can only be tricked if you are open to it. And if you're open to it, that means you were looking for something, and fuck, we're *all* looking for something! Bottom line: Have you ever had catfish? Fried up in a po'boy?! What?! That shit is delicious! So the way I see it, when it comes to catfish, just make sure you're the one doing the cooking! Pick out a nice catfish, fillet that shit, and remove all the bones—you don't want to choke on a catfish bone! Clean the fish, dip it in some egg wash, then in some salted and seasoned bread crumbs, then fry that muthafucka golden brown, throw on some hot sauce, and voilà!

I know, I just gave you a recipe for actual catfish (a damn good ass recipe). I don't want you thinking I don't know what the fuck an online catfish is. I have a recipe for that one too. First of all, you need a fake profile and you need to fill it with fake interests; I call that shit the bait. Use the type of bait that you need to attract the type of fish you want. Don't talk about whips and chains and shit in your profile, unless you intend to do some or have your ass whipped. I won't go on about interests 'cause I think most people get that part right. Where people fuck up is the picture, or should I say fake picture. Now, I'm not against the fake picture, but I think people back themselves into a corner with their selection. Most people pick the picture of someone way more attractive than themselves, and that's fine if you never want to meet the person. But I'm Leon damn Black: I'm online to fuck, not fuck around!

So, here's how you pick a picture! Say you are looking to hook up with some artsy type: Load up your profile with a bunch of works of art, and if you don't know any, go to a fucking museum and do your homework—you'll find this trip useful. While you're there, look at some art, get some culture, learn a little something. Think you can't? One day I stared at the *Mona Lisa* for damn near three hours just to try to figure out what that smug ass lady was thinking! See, she's a quintessential woman, kind of like one of my aunties. She's like this aunt of mine who comes to family reunions and always has that "I'm better than you" face on. Maybe she has a different father than everyone else or went to some fancy school so she thinks she can sit in the corner eating banana pudding while judging everyone. That's that *Mona Lisa* look. It's complex, a lot of ladies rock it, hard as fuck to read. Not like this other painting I stared at, this one called *The Scream*—that creepy ass lady's face is straightforward as fuck! And haunting! That painting reminds me of a lady with a three-feet restraining order: So, Peaches, if you're reading this book, that constitutes a violation of the order, so put it down and step four feet back.

Back to the picture: While you're there, remember some works of art to use in your profile, and then—and most important—find a handsome security guard or tour guide and discreetly snap his picture. That is the picture you use on your profile! Then over the next few days case the place like you're a bank robber from one of those heist movies. Have yourself a little pad and pencil and take notes of that security guard or that tour guide's schedule; you will need this info. Once you finish that process, go home, set up your catfishing bait, and wait for the fish! Once you get one, reel that shit in! Based on the schedule from your notes, make a date to meet at that museum, let her know you work there, and tell her to look for you because you'll be waiting. Then go to that museum, go to the snack bar and get some snacks, find a good spot, and wait. See, now you're in a position to see your catfish before she sees you. Watch that damn tour guide and notice the expressions of the people who approach him. Sooner or later some nervous ass woman dressed to impress will awkwardly approach him. If she's a train wreck or looks like she narrowly survived one, cut your losses and leave. But if she's attractive, slowly make your way over. What's gonna happen is that she's gonna come up to him with a whole bunch of stuff to say, and he's gonna be like, "What the fuck's going on?!" You know, all confused and shit. At that point, you should be within ear range so that you can offer some comforting words, like "I don't mean to be rude, but I was overhearing what's going on. It appears to me that this beautiful lady has been catfished, and I think that's awful, just awful." Definitely hit her with the double "awful." See, she will be so vulnerable and embarrassed that she'll eat your kindness up. Then say some shit like it might be a bad day for her, but as for you, "I came here to see some works of art, and lucky for me you walked in!" Trust me, you'll be fucking by nightfall! Damn, I love me some fried catfish!

DISNEYLAND
AND WORLD

$\mathfrak{H}$ ere's my philosophy on fake ass thrills: some people need them, but I don't! I deal in real thrills, ones that have a payoff!

Wanna know what a real thrill sounds like? A real thrill is shit like putting your name on a waiting list for that space shuttle trip to Mars! Or going all cryogenic and freezing your ass for the future like Walt damn Disney. That was one interesting man. That crazy ass visionary created Disney World, and Disney World freaks me the fuck out. Now, I'm not trying to discourage anyone from partaking of the Disney empire, be it Disneyland, Disney World, Disney Cruise, Disney Island, Disney Universe, or whatever the fuck they have, because I would have no problem dropping my nieces and nephews off and picking them up later. I know they would enjoy the fuck out of it because for kids Disney is magic—it's just not for me. I just don't like costumed people dancing around and shit when I don't know who the fuck is underneath.

Plus I get thrown off by the logistics of shit. See, I'm a very logistical thinker, and when the reality of shit is out of whack I get thrown off immediately. For instance, the fact that Mickey and Minnie are mice and are supposed to be way smaller than Goofy, who is a dog, and yet they are all the same size—see the proportions are off . . . logistics.

Not to mention that Goofy and Pluto are both dogs, but Pluto is a real dog on a leash, while Goofy walks and talks and shit. Being Goofy does not exclude the fact that you're a dog. You telling me that they never had a beef as to why Pluto is on a fucking leash? Is Goofy just a dog walker for Pluto, 'cause that's fucked up. Or is Pluto just the sex slave in the scenario?! If Goofy wants to keep it real, he should be walking on all fours. That's commitment to your fucking job.

That being said, I love me some goddamn Minnie Mouse, with her short ass skirt showing a little hint of panty and her big ass shoes. She's clearly a beautiful black woman with just a touch of vitiligo around her face; that's a sexy lady. And she's got her own place. Shit, if I went to Disney, I'd fuck around and have Mickey catch me at her place coming out of her bedroom in a Disney souvenir towel, one of those ones with Tinkle Bell flying over the castle shooting off that sparkly shit . . . that little bitch ain't bad either, sticking her little booty out all the time, waving that little wand, she could catch it! Anyway, I would be like, "You better lock that rodent ass down, Mickey!" See, I don't get their relationship. It's not like they're married. They are both single, but nobody ever talks about that shit. Nobody ever says, "Is Minnie your wife?" "No, she's my side bitch." Which is the truth, of course, but he can't say that in front of the kids. So he just says, "She's my friend."

I mean, don't get me wrong, I know kids have fun at Disney, but don't kids deserve the truth? I'm sure Walt would have agreed.

SOUPED-UP

These days people love themselves some damn superheroes! I'm not gonna lie, man, I love that shit too, I dream about that stuff all the time! Who wouldn't want to be a damn superhero? There's so many of them I like that I can't pick a favorite. To be honest, I'm already kind of a superhero myself because I have a superpower: I have the power of persuasion. You understand what that is, right? I have to the ability to talk a man *into* believing in me, and talk a lady *out of* her panties. That shit is a gift, the gift of gab! Superman couldn't do that! Batman couldn't do that! Then again, that muthafucka is a bad ass millionaire, he might be able to do that—shit, he is the Dark Knight!

Like I said, I already have a superpower, but if I was gonna add some more abilities, here's what I would want:

1. Density—I would look like myself, normal appearance, but I would be as fuckin' heavy as an elephant. If I caused trouble in a restaurant over some cold soup and security came to remove me, they wouldn't be able to budge me. And don't fuck around

and make me step on your damn foot—I would flatten your
shit. One problem, though: I would have to shit standing up
'cause I would break any toilet if I sat down. I'm sayin' I would
be fucking solid! Also, like an elephant I would have an excellent
memory, I would be my own villain database; they all would be
in my head. My only weakness: mice.

2. Flight—I would have the power of flight but I would only be
able to fly two feet off the ground; see, I'm afraid of heights. It
would work out well, though, because being on street level would
help me be able to see shit with more detail. I would have the
ability to find small shit like contact lenses. Do you know the
kind of evidence I could find?! A chewed-up piece of gum, bullet
fragments, shiiiit! Plus if you fly two feet off the ground, you
are more accessible to ladies; you would be there right at waist
level making it easy to flirt and get some numbers. Also, if a
muthafucka owed you some money, you could fly right at pocket
level and chase him down till he paid up. My only weakness:
parked cars, fences, hydrants, parking meters, Great Danes, bags
of garbage, dwarfs—actually too many obstacles to list, so I'll
just say et cetera.

3. Overhearing—It's not that I would have great hearing, it's that
I would always be in the right place to overhear shit. Good shit,
bad shit, bullshit—I would be able to hear it all. Also, I would
have selective hearing, which means I would have the ability to
only overhear the shit that I wanted to, meaning I would be able
to focus on one specific thing and block out the rest. Do you
know how cool that it is? Other superheroes with superhearing
have to listen to everything, all kinds of bullshit, but not the
kid. My only weakness: a muthafucka catching me all up in his
business.

4. Shadowing—I could turn into your shadow on the ground, that way I could follow you without you knowing. And if you made love to your lady outdoors in the sun, I would fuck the shit out of your lady's shadow. My weakness: obviously, darkness.

5. Vision—See, 'cause my last name is Black, I would have Black Light vision. I would be able to see all types shit, DNA, cum, semen—I think those three are the same but I still had to mention each one of them. Also, I would see piss, urine, fecal matter, bodily fluids . . . I would be able to see all that mess on walls, on floors, on ceilings, on people, yes on fucking people! My weakness: dirty ass hotel rooms. What? As useful as that power would be, do you understand the curse that comes along with it? The world is a filthy fuckin' place! Imagine staying in a hotel room if you had Black Light vision? Seeing all the shit that's splattered all over that damn hotel bathroom? And the mattress!?! Don't get me started on that! That's why I would have to wear a utility belt filled with super cleaning products so that I could clean shit up for my own sanity! All kinds of cleaning products, Kaboom, Mr. Clean, sponges, Handi Wipes, a retractable Swiffer! All that shit! That being said, I would be able to solve the fuck out of some crimes!

CAMP FUCKTHAT

Someone suggested I watch some show called *Naked and Afraid*. I figured it had "naked" in the title, so it was worth me checking it out. On the show, they put a sexy couple of naked strangers in the forest and they challenge them to survive the elements for twenty-one days. I watched the first ten minutes of the show and thought to myself that the hardest part of this show wouldn't be to survive nature for twenty-one days. No, the hardest part for me would be to not bring the ruckus to that sexy naked ass stranger. I'm like, "How do these people not have sex all day long?" Until I started to realize those naked people don't have any soap, any damn toilet paper—that's why those nasty ass naked people don't fuck.

With the idea of fucking out of the way, I just sat there and watched these people try to survive. Throughout the show, all these two filthy naked ass people did was complain about how hard things were. Hard to survive in nature? Are you kidding me? Sitting there worried about some wild animals? Why? What's that animal gonna do to you? Eat you? Maybe, but at least that's all he wants to do. An animal's motives are straightforward, which is easy to navigate. Now, a person—any person—is way scarier to me than any damn animal! People commit premeditated crimes, animals don't. I have never heard of a raccoon taking a person's wallet at gunpoint. You will never read about a kangaroo stealing someone's identity and using it to get a credit card, go on Amazon, and buy a Fire TV Stick. Man, I watch this other show, *The First 48*. On that show, you see a detective trying to solve a murder within forty-eight hours. Not once on that show have I ever seen them bring a warthog in for questioning, not once. Now, I did read online about a silverback gorilla that tore a man's face off. But as horrible a crime as that was, it doesn't compare to the time I heard about a man who meticulously cut this other man's face off and was caught wearing it when he got pulled over driving the man's Jeep Cherokee. Give me a damn animal any day.

TIME TRAVEL AGENT

Anyone who wants to travel back in time is a stupid ass motherfucker. Who the fuck would want to go back and see shit that's already happened? The only reason to travel back in time is after you've gone forward, and that's just so you can get back to where you were. No, I want to see some new shit. I would love to visit the future, but just for a quick look. I wouldn't want to spoil the surprise for myself. I want to see how ladies conduct themselves in the future. What outfits are they gonna have on? Futuristic movies have told us for years that people will be wearing metallic spandex jumpsuits and shit. I'm hoping that's the case. I'm hoping the future is like it was in another one of my favorite movies, *The Fifth Element*. Woo, that movie turned me on! What?!! Milla Jovovich was sexy as hell in that movie! You damn right I remember her name! Crazy thing, I don't remember the names of people in my life, but I damn sure remember the names of actors in my favorite movies! Rounding out that damn film, my man Bruce Willis, my dude Chris Tucker, and the man who always plays a good ass bad guy, Gary Oldman!

I'm telling you, I love that movie! Milla was so damn sexy—simple but sexy. She spoke very few words, no nagging, no complaining; she said everything with her eyes. I could definitely get with a woman like that! Now, I'm not saying I could live the rest of my life with a woman like that, though. I mean, I'm sure she would be a pain in the ass when we're trying to pick a place to go to dinner, but I guess there's a trade-off in every relationship.

One crazy thing, though: That movie about the future was made back in 1997 . . . Ain't that some shit? The future movie is now an old part of movie history. I still love the way they made the world look. See, that's why I would love to go into the future and then come right back. I just wanna visit long enough to see how people party. And fly damn cars—*Fifth Element* has flying cars all over the place. Since they started making movies about the future, they've been showing us flying cars. You might ask yourself, "When are we actually gonna get ourselves some flying cars?" I'll tell you—when ignorance is abolished. Really, think about that shit! With all the crazy people in the world, would you really want the average person to have access to a flying car? Besides the terrible accidents, can you imagine the road rage? Two people crash and one hops out of his car to talk some shit, forgets he's in the air, and falls two thousand feet to his death. Or better yet, since it's the future, he gets out of his car, turns on his jetpack, and hovers over to the other car to curse that dude out . . . which leads me to this question about the future: Why would someone with a flying car be wearing a fucking jetpack? Doesn't make any sense, does it? And that's exactly why I wouldn't stay in the future!

OLD AGE

COUGARLAND

𝕴've tapped some old ass ladies. Plenty. People call them "cougars." I don't. First thing I think about when I hear the word "cougar" is a Buick or a Pontiac or whoever manufactured that fucking car in the 1970s. I'll tell you the biggest perk of tapping old ass ladies: They doze off early. You don't have to siphon off the entire evening. You make love to an old ass lady and then let them doze off while you do the other shit in the meantime: watch basketball, or if you're at her house, you can do laundry and shit. I'm not talking about any old lady, I'm talking about the ones that took care of themselves. Sometimes while they're sleeping, the grandkids are gonna call. And then you gotta tell them, "Sorry, Johnnie, Grandma is sleeping." "Why?" they'll ask. And you gotta be honest: "Because I tore your grandma's ass up. I'ma be honest with you, your grandma's fast, meaning she's vivacious and she can hang with a man half her age." Now, don't let anyone tell you that's bad parenting, 'cause you're not their parent, you're just the dude tapping their old grandma.

I don't want you to think I just take from old people, I also give back. I used to give lectures at old-age homes about how to get laid. On another subject in my experience, I've noticed that old folks' homes either ironically have "Shady" or "Sunny" in their name. And don't quote me, but the old people at the Sunny ones seem happy and energetic, while the ones in the Shady ones seem sneaky, unhappy, and vindictive. It's not like I did a study or anything, I'm just saying.

One thing I would preach to those old people is the importance of stretching. What I told those old ass people goes for anyone over fifty reading this book: Stretch every part of your body. I'm serious, I cannot emphasize this enough. If you can't stretch yourself, have a buddy stretch you for you. The last thing y'all need is to pull a muscle in the middle of fucking. You're already both at risk for heart attacks, slipped discs, and strokes. Try to minimize the risk and just move your body around a bit, simulate the back and forth of fucking if you have to.

For anyone under fifty reading this book, you might be surprised to know that if you can get past all the clicking and cracking sounds, old people are pretty damn flexible. It's easy to understand why, though: Old people love going to classes. They love themselves some tai chi and yoga! Oh, and mall walking. They really love the fuck out of some mall walking! They get up early, put on some old Al Sharpton or Tony Soprano jogging suits, and walk briskly around a mall. They move their arms like they're running, but the fact is they are walking, slow as shit. The irony is that some people call sexy old women "cougars," but I ain't never seen a cougar walk that damn slow!

I wish old people did have the characteristics of a real ass cougar, though. Criminals would think twice about mugging a sweet little old lady if they had to worry about being mauled by her.

VINTAGE
SEX POSITIONS

Don't get it twisted! The internet would have you believe freaky sex shit is new. Hell, your grandparents were filthy! You're having a hard time believing your grandparents were beatin' it up?! I've got a whole list of shit Percy and Bernadette were doing back in the day. Now sure, the Cotton Gin, the Wheelbarrow, and the Reverse Wheelbarrow are so famous they can be found in Urban Dictionary. But there are some lesser-known ones that were pretty damn good:

◆ **Donkey Style:** Just like doggie style, except when the woman was done, she double-foot kicked the man in the chest to get him off her. People were busy back then, they didn't have time to lie around for some post-coital cuddling.

◆ **Polio:** When the woman acted like her legs didn't work. You know how much fun you could have working the dead legs? Hours. Hours, I'm telling you! I know that shit is dark, and no offense to any physically challenged individuals out there. On the contrary, I know you've been doing kinky ass shit for years and not sharing it with us, so kudos to you!

- **Model T:** A rough hand job, where the Johnson was rotated like a crank. Hey, don't judge. People liked that rough shit back then—it matched the times.
- **Woody Woodpecker:** Like a blowjob, but from a woman with buck teeth and a nervous ass laugh.
- **Fried Baloney:** The lady sat her ass on a stove top and turned it on low heat, then the man kept sliding his Johnson in between her and the stove top until they both smelled liked fried baloney. That one was fucked up, but fun! That one kept the ER busy.

There were also a few racist ones that never caught on, for instance:

- **The Colored Fountain:** This was when a black woman would pee on a chocolate-loving white man. While colored fountains were legal in the South, ironically the Colored Fountain Shower was not. Shit, I don't wanna even tell you what would happen if they caught you peeing on someone of another race. Shit was bad back then, on all levels. It would be some time later, after many years of illegal interracial sex peeing, that golden showers would be born. I'm telling you facts here!

SPEAKING OF
OLD ASS PEOPLE

𝕴've always been told, as you get older, don't be so picky when it comes to picking a partner, because the last thing you want to do is grow old alone. I get it. Nobody wants to end up old and alone. I'm a meat eater, and lemme tell you, people should never eat meat alone. Especially your dark meats! Meats like beef, lamb, goat, bison, bear, wild boar. Now don't confuse a wild boar with a pig. A wild boar is stubborn and stuck in its ways, which causes it to have some tough meat, while on the other hand pigs are indecisive. Shit, I read a story where three of them muthafuckas couldn't decide what to build their house out of: twigs, straw, or bricks. What kind of fucking choice is that? And really, with all the affordable developments and nice gated communities out there, why build at all? At least make that wolf have to check in at security and ride an elevator before he eats you.

Trust me, pigs and boars may look a little alike, but they are very different. Picture a little pig in a laboratory: he's got his little lab coat on, test tubes everywhere; that little pig is doing some kind of pig experiments. At some point that pig takes a sip of some blue or green liquid from one of those test tubes, and all of a sudden that pig starts gasping and squealing and shit, and then takes his hooves and knocks over all the test tubes. For a second that pig disappears under the table, and when he pops back up, he's got tusks, coarse ass whiskers, and he's wearing a top hat and a cape . . . that motherfucka is a wild boar. A pig is Dr. Jekyll and a wild boar is Mr. Hyde. You may enjoy a nice, tender Jekyll chop, but trust me, you will choke to death on some Mr. Hyde ribs.

My point is dark, heavy meats will cause an old person to choke, and if you're old and alone, that could be a death sentence. If you do end up old and alone and feel like you have to have some meat, focus on safe meats like Spam, deviled ham, Vienna sausages—pretty much all the potted meats (shit that looks like someone ate it already, then regurgitated it into a small can, like a bird). By the way, I bet a lot of you don't even know what the fuck a Vienna sausage is. That's because it's what sausages do; a sausage comes around and people are all into it but then another sausage comes up behind it and takes its place. It's just like immigrants—how the Germans came here, then the Polish, then the Italians; each ethnicity had their time. Coincidentally, each one of those is a sausage, and that's my point. See, no one remembers when the Viennans came to America, but trust me, they came and brought their little ass sausages with them. Now while they were good as hors d' oeuvres, they overstepped when they tried to grab the pigs in a blanket market and the mini hot dog shut them down. Also, their bigger problems were they were too mushy and too damn small; you try to put them on the grill and they just fall right through the grate.

Take note: Having someone around when you're old doesn't guarantee you're gonna survive a choking. There are skills involved. That person needs to be able to form a fist (arthritis and gout could make that difficult), and they must be able to take that fist and pound the shit out of your back to dislodge that dark ass meat. Fucking Heimlich maneuver is bullshit. The only thing that works is the pound on the back maneuver. But just like how Vaseline beat the shit out of all other petroleum jellies, marketing is the key. The Heimlich maneuver, invented in 1974 by Dr. Henry Heimlich, was able to get its damn informative instructional diagrams in every restaurant there is, while the pound on the back maneuver's diagram was shunned by most establishments because the sign just looked like one guy was beating the shit out of another guy. Plus, on top of everything there would also be a concern about the possibility of lawsuits. By the way, if you are ever taken to court for breaking some old man's back while trying to save him, I suggest you try the "I Didn't Know My Own Strength" defense. Many people don't know their own strength. Actually, this is a universal defense. Like when you're helping some random chick you hooked up with at the Frozen Yogurt Hut back into her dress and you break that little damn zipper. Seems specific but it happens a lot, trust me. It's always much easier to help a lady out of her clothes than to help her back in . . . physically, that is; mentally it's the other way around. I know this one got a little off track, but basically to sum up, if you're old, eat soft shit, cut it up into small pieces, have someone chew it for you, preferably a grandchild— they are young and would probably get a kick out of spitting a wad of meat onto your plate. Bottom line is don't eat shit you can't swallow, you old fucks. Too much?

SINGLE-SERVING SENIORS

Old muthafuckas get moldy. Just like bread. When I see an old muthafucka buying a big ass loaf of bread, I want to tell him to let me buy that loaf 'cause his old ass isn't gonna live long enough to eat that whole loaf. But if I said that I would be wrong. Not to be mean, but in general old people should only buy small portions. And don't buy a pack of razors; open that pack up and take one out. Trust me, the salesperson wouldn't say a thing. Every time I see an old person at Costco, I wanna be like, "What the fuck are you doing here? You don't need to buy your shit in bulk. What are you, eighty-five? Don't waste your goddamn money at Costco." I want to say shit like that, but I know if I did say it—the truth, mind you—I would be wrong, so I don't say a word.

Instead, though, I'll follow an old man like that around just to see what kind of other excessive shit he's gonna buy. As I do, I'm quietly hoping this old man is not gonna pick up one of those giant cartons of 144 eggs. Fuck around and bring all those damn eggs home and have them there so long those damn things hatch. Think they won't? When you were in elementary school, did you ever have to help out with one of those incubators that they use to hatch an egg? All you really had to do was shine that hot ass lightbulb on it, and that damn chicken would pop out of that egg. Now, if a lightbulb can hatch one adorable baby chick, then how many baby chicks would an old person's hot ass house bring into this world?!? There'd be 144 damn adorable chicks running around the house. And you know how old people are with shit. You would be like, "Pop, there are baby chicks running around the house!" And Pop would say something simple, like "What chicks?" And trust me, that exchange will stay the same for a while, 'cause Pop will never see those damn baby chicks. A baby chick's feet move too fast, and old man Pop's eyes move too slow.

Of course, two weeks later, after he's dead and his grandkids are cleaning out his house, going through his fridge and the freezer and what not, they will wonder why the fuck Pop had thirty-six loaves of bread, four hundred rolls of toilet paper, a barrel of mustard, an eight-month supply of Efferdent, and a bunch of nasty ass chickens running around. See, by that time, those adorable ass chicks have turned into nasty ass chickens, and let me tell you something, chickens will fuck up a house in a heartbeat.

JIFFY LUBE FOR SENIORS

Think of life as like a NASCAR race: Every now and then you need to pull your ass in for a pit stop and get your shit checked out. Check your mechanics, check your tires, but most important, check your damn fluids! Do you know how much can be learned about you from your damn pee? You learn the most from your pee!

Peeing is an art that we take for granted. I don't recommend this, but as I mentioned in the Flu Dick section, I wash my hands before I pee so I can eat a sandwich while I'm peeing . . . but I don't know where your hands or, for that matter, your Johnson has been so I can't speak for you. Men don't have to think when we pee, we pee as we go. Honestly, all you need is a ten- to twenty-second window and you can literally relieve yourself anywhere. I used to pee in cups, but now I pee in Gatorade bottles all the time.

The capacity of my bladder exactly matches that of an eight-ounce Gatorade bottle, but that took years of experimentation to know. Before the Gatorade bottle I tried shit like Big Gulps, a Red Bull can, a baby bottle (don't ask), and a rain boot. Starbucks cups were helpful—I tried the Tall, the Venti, and the Grande—and one time at a luau I peed in a gutted-out pineapple. Don't judge me, I've been in a lot of desperate pee situations.

A weak bladder and no shame will do that to you. Doctors tell you that to strengthen your bladder you should practice stopping your pee flow three or four times while urinating, but that shit is impossible. Once I start peeing I can't stop, and trust me, that can be a problem, especially when you are in your car trying to pee into a sixteen-ounce Mountain Dew bottle, which by the way is an art in itself! Do you understand how accurate you have to be to get your pee into that little opening—especially while you're driving?!

Let me tell you something, I'm a goddamn sharpshooter. After all of my experiments were done, I had discovered all I needed to know about my accuracy and my capacity. That's some important shit. 'Cause the last thing you wanna find out while you're driving is that your pee capacity is way more than eight or sixteen ounces and you pee all over your car seat upholstery, especially if you try to sell that car one day. I'm telling you, no matter how much you shampoo that interior, that car will always have a hint of dirty aquarium water smell . . . well, maybe just mine.

KAPUT

𝕴 was torn as to what I was gonna call this section. See, this chapter is about funerals, but I figured if you knew that right away, you would skip on ahead to the next chapter. Several titles ran through my head—"Death," "Funeral"—and I was really leaning toward "My Friend, You Out This Bitch," but I went with "Kaput" because I knew most of you wouldn't know what the fuck "Kaput" meant.

Look here, you can't avoid funerals; sooner or later we're all gonna have one. Unless of course you're some kind of mob informant who they tied to a cinder block and tossed into Lake Deep as Fuck. Even then, if you have loved ones, you'll probably still have a funeral, only your body just won't be there. There will just be some dumb ass photo of you in the casket. If you ask me, they should put a mannequin in there with your picture taped to the face.

And that's my point—funerals are too damn sad, and something needs to be done about it. A funeral should have a best man. Unlike the wedding situation, a best man is fine in this situation because you're already dead, so there is no chance to be upstaged. There is the slight danger that he could flirt with your grieving widow. Which is fucked up, but whatchu gonna do about it?

Have your best man or lady set up the funeral, set up the whole thing, and make it fun. Make it like an Easter egg hunt. Have them paint you in some bright colors and hide your ass somewhere. Offer prizes for the folks who find you. The prizes could be shit that while you were alive they wanted to borrow but you always said no. A little fucked up? Maybe, but again, whatchu gonna do? Anyway, make the hunt a challenge. Give clues and shit. Make it fun! Just don't make it too hard to find you, 'cause if they don't—just like one of them eggs—you will start stinking.

These days I only go to the destination funerals, where I can get over my depression with some sunbathing or interesting sight-seeing. Someone die in NJ? Fuck that, but a funeral in Sedona or Napa Valley? Where they've got them wine tastings with all them delicious wines like Cabs and Zinfandels and Pinot Grigios? I'm a bit of a connoisseur—I love me some wine! I just don't like wineglasses—that's why I drink it straight out of the box.

After I'm gone, though, I don't want a bunch of people coming up there to say shit about me. I don't care what anyone else has to say about me, I care what I have to say about me. I want people to quote me and say shit like "If I may draw from *The Book of Leon*" or "In the immortal words of Leon Black." See, that shit there sets you apart from just about everyone. It puts you in an exclusive group, muthafuckas like Plato, Socrates. I would never draw from Confucius, though. He just sounds confused. It's right there in his goddamn name! To be honest, I bet his real name was Stuart.

WORDS TO
LIVE BY

MISSION IMPOSSIBLE

There are three things that supposedly good parents tell their kids. One, parents are programmed to tell their kids that they are beautiful. Now that may seem like a good thing, but in all actuality that parent is just setting that damn kid up. Most likely that kid is ugly, statistically speaking, so the only chance that little muthafucka has is that whole "beauty is in the eye of the beholder" shit. The problem with that is the fucked up–looking kid will have to spend his life looking for the beholder while the rest of the world beholds his ugly ass. Now if you have a pretty child I'm not speaking to you, but if you have an ugly child, which you probably do, by telling that little mongrel muthafucka he's handsome you are sending him down a long, lonely road.

The second thing these irresponsible ass parents do is tell their kids they're "special." Now while some shit like that is damaging, it's not as bad as the first one, because over the years "special" has lost some of its glamour. I mean, you can order the Two for Tuesday—two eggs, two sausages, two bacon, two pancakes, to-go "special." Hell, I knew a kid in school who was "special," and that muthafucka used to misspell his damn name constantly . . . and his fucking name was Ed. Now you might think it, but I can't blame that shit on the teacher—that's some parenting shit.

All that being said by far the worst thing your parent could ever do to you is tell you that you can do anything as long as you put your mind to it, 'cause that is some bullshit! In life there will always be stuff that is out of reach. You think when I'm sitting on Larry's couch I'm worrying about shit I can't do? I'm really thinking about shit I can do. Stuff like: go in his refrigerator and eat the chicken salad that he took the time to label "Larry," use his dumb electric car and use up all the damn charge, or fuck some bitches in his king-size bed and not change the sheets, or urinate in all his bathrooms—hell, Larry's got like five different bathrooms. Trust me, there are days that I make sure to consume enough liquids to pee in every one of them. Realize in life there are things that you just can't do—it's the circle of life . . . if I may quote one of my favorite ass Disney films *The Lion King*. To be honest, now that I think about it, I might have used that quote in the wrong context. It probably really has more to do with an impala or a gazelle being eaten by a lion, or like a spider eating a fly or some shit, but no matter what, I think you still get my point. My advice: Don't think too hard out about your shortcomings, because if you do, you will spend the rest of your life stressed out about the shit you can't do! Let it go! For example, if you have arachnophobia, you can't be Spider-Man. How you gonna be scared of yourself and save the fucking world? Another example: You are not gonna be a ballerina if you've got fat feet. Note that I did not say fat people couldn't be ballerinas, I said fat-footed people couldn't. There are plenty of skinny people with fat feet, just like there are a lot of fat people with skinny feet. In any event, none of those muthafuckas could be ballerinas. And until the Association for Disproportionately Footed People makes a big deal about my stance, I stand by what the fuck I just said, so come and get me. I'll be right here waiting. And you're lucky I'll be waiting, because if I ran, there's no way in hell you disproportionately footed muthafuckas could ever catch me! Like I said, some things in life are impossible. Shall I continue?

FOUR-LEGGED RACE

You see a guy like me and a guy like Larry riding by on a tandem bike, the first thing you might think to yourself is, *What the fuck are those two dudes doing riding one of those bikes together?*

But I tell you, the question you should be asking is how do you turn that bitch? Trust me, a tandem bike? That shit ain't easy to ride. That shit requires teamwork and trust. The two of you need to be joined at the hip like Siamese twins. Scientifically speaking, your body displacement needs to be in sync. To be honest, it's easier to ride a tandem bike by yourself—the second person just usually throws you off, they are more of a nuisance than anything else. See, that's why me and Larry make a great team. Despite how we look or sound, we work well together and we could definitely ride the fuck out of one of those bikes, that is, as long as I sit up front. Fuck that, I ain't gonna let no man ride me around, I ain't no punk. Plus, I wouldn't trust Larry to steer—if you've ever seen Larry's glasses, you know he's blind as fuck.

The world has gotten so divided these days. The messed-up thing is that people use race and religion to group people up, but I'm here to tell you we are all more alike than you know. Really, there are only two types of people: the fuckers who have the time to parasail on a random Tuesday afternoon, and the fuckers who don't. If you are the kind of person who sometimes searches for some shit to do on a Tuesday and parasailing comes into the equation, you are clearly living a good ass life! You must have some dummy money, a shitload of properties, and a ton of other shit except problems. Then there's the other group. I don't have to describe the other group, 'cause you know what the fuck I'm talking about.

See what I did there? I broke the world down into two types of people with no mention of race. Although, to be fair, most times when you see one of those Tuesday parasailors, they're super white. But that is not to say that you could never see a black person up there! I would just say that if you do, take a quick look at the ground below him, 'cause you just might see the white girl he's fucking driving the speedboat. No disrespect!

BUFFETARIAN

Every religion has its legitimate parts and its crazy ass parts, but I don't judge, 'cause the crazy parts help people take in the legitimate parts. I'm a religious buffetarian. I take a little bit of everything from everybody, because at the end of the day, religion is supposed to help people. Leonism is a religion, and a damn good one. But you don't see me plastering myself on walls of buildings or stained-glass windows. Because I'm humble.

And I believe my disciples should have their own face as their God, 'cause believing in yourself is what makes you powerful. It's what allows you to bring the ruckus. So you can adopt my tenets and my beliefs and make them your own.

Sure, I've gone through phases where I said, "Leon, make yourself some fucking bumper stickers, or make a bunch of cookies with your face on them, sneak into Nabisco or some shit and mix your cookies into a box of that Keebler Elves' shit so that people around the world can find your image in their Keebler Elf cookie box. All you need is one in each box, but you have to put your shit into a lot of boxes, because most people will just wind up eating your cookie and never seeing your face. Trust me, that kind of publicity works! People see religious images in everything—toast, burnt pancake, Cheetos, tater tots, pizza, Cinnabons, cappuccino . . . not just food, though: clouds, trees, the knots on the back of someone's head—trust me, if people are looking for religious images, they will find them everywhere. So spread your gospel, and get credit for it.

But then I realized that's my ego talking, not my divine spirit and self. So myself says, "Fuck that, I don't need people following me everywhere, this God has some very un-Godly shit to do, and I damn sure don't need nobody watching me."

Trust me, it's better to be a God figure that's off the grid than to have your disciples all up in your damn scriptures.

Leonism is spreading at a phenomenal rate, and before long, I know I'm gonna get phone calls from pissed-off religious leaders all over the world. Rabbis, priests, reverends—shit, I know Oprah's gonna call to debunk Leonism on Super Soul Sunday . . . Then the Dalai Lama's probably gonna call me and be like, "Leon, my brother, what are you doing? I've been working hard without even having my own country as a base to spread the word of kindness and compassion around the world, and you're f*#king it all up for me!"

WHAT I SAY—
WHAT I MEAN

WORD ARTIST

Here's the thing: I like to think of myself as a word artist. Most artists stare at a blank canvas until an idea hits them, and then they create art. I like to think that the brain of the person in front of me is a blank canvas, and my job as an artist is to look into the eyes of that damn blank canvas and light that shit up! Sometimes I'm thinking more classic like a Rembrandt or a Michael Angelo, but other times I'm more like a graffiti artist! Sometimes I make muscum-quality shit, and sometimes my shit is like the stuff you see on a subway car or a bathroom stall or way up on a damn billboard. You know those ones way up there, the ones you look at like, how the fuck did the guy get up there?! When you see shit up there like that, it usually says something like "Fuck Karen!" Which always makes me wonder, like, *Damn, what did Karen do to make a muthafucka so mad that he would risk his damn life to climb way the fuck up there and make sure she sees it on her way to work?!* Stuff like that makes you question every Karen you meet from that point on, 'cause the last thing you want to do is to get stuck with *that* damn Karen. Now, sometimes I go back and forth and feel bad for Karen, and all Karens, for that matter. See, the problem is muthafuckas never put the damn last name, or at least, if you're a damn artist, draw a picture of Karen! It's just too confusing, even for other Karens who see it and wonder to themselves *Am I that damn Karen!?* In turn they start calling up exes and yelling at their asses to see if they put that shit up there! See, not identifying which Karen it is is some selfish shit! What you've done is created a Karen virus—every Karen thinks it's them, and everyone who dated a Karen thinks they dated *the* Karen. Do you understand how messed-up that is? Karens are mothers, daughters, granddaughters, teachers, nuns! There are babies who could've been born Karen but their mothers drove by that damn sign and now they have to second-guess themselves! Did you know that in 1965 Karen was the third-most popular name in America, but as of 2016 it's only ranked 504th? That's over a 500 percent drop! See what the fuck you did!

Now, what the fuck was I just talking about?

Oh yeah, I'm a word artist! Yeah, once I open my mouth, I just create. Half the time I don't think about what I'm saying, it just comes out! And like most art, if you try to understand it before it's finished, you would be like, "What the fuck is that?!" But by the time I'm done, you will definitely know what the fuck I'm talking about . . . unless you are dumb as shit!

Now, usually after I'm done saying something, I don't remember it at all; this is a skill I developed called "plausible deniability." But sometimes the thing that I said is so profound that people start quoting me and making t-shirts out of my shit to capitalize on my brilliant ass word art! By the way, Fuck Karen t-shirts will be available just in time for the holidays. I'll keep you posted.

BRING THE RUCKUS

People think "ruckus" is causing commotion. It's not. I myself am a "Bringer of Ruckus," with "Bringer" being the key ass word! See, I bring it but I don't cause it; that's a big difference. If you cause shit, you can be liable, and liability opens you up to fines, lawsuits, and jail time.

For instance, you go to a petting zoo and start talking shit and fucking with the animals, trying to ride a mule, or worse yet a goat—you know, animals that you ain't supposed to ride, a penguin, a snake, shit like that. You are causing a ruckus, and your ass is going to jail. But if that same goddamn billy goat followed you to a party and started tearing shit up, baa-baa-ing, shitting on the floor, stepping on the couch, putting his dirty ass hoofs in the punchbowl and randomly drop kicking muthafuckas in the chest, I mean really fucking somebody's birthday party up and some lady screams, more than likely the birthday girl screams, "Oh my God whose goat is this!?! He's fucking my party up! Why is he only kicking black people!?" Sure you brought that Ruckus with you, but all that shit is on the racist ass goat and the people who threw the party and decided to let him in. I bring the Ruckus, but if you get kicked in the chest, that's on you!

GET IN THAT ASS

IT'S EASY TO GET IN THAT ASS—
IT'S NOT ALWAYS EASY TO GET OUT

It is pretty damn easy to get in that ass. You get angry enough, you'll get in that ass! Caught up defending yourself? Argument with your significant other? If you're not careful, you will wind up in that ass! It happens. What is "getting in that ass," you ask? It is a verbal form of ass whupping. It is a way of defending yourself or your lady. To master it is to master the art of talking a good game. And when you're good at it, it can be more devastating than a sucker punch. Now, me? I purposely get in that ass! It is what I do! I do it out of anger or just for the fun of it! I have been in many asses! And no one is safe from an ass entering! A boss, a grandma, a police officer . . . Larry! I don't care. Sometimes it takes people a while to get in that ass; not me, I'll get up in that ass and start a small fire.

Getting in an ass is easy, but getting out, that's another thing! Too many people get into an ass without an exit strategy. Let me tell you something: Don't just run up in an ass! You might wind up like a little kid running into a forest and then looking back, like, "Where the fuck am I?" Asses are like those walk-through haunted houses: It's easy to get in—you just buy a fuckin' ticket—but once you're in and you start walking around, you get distracted by monsters and goblins and shit! You're in that haunted ass, and before you know it, you've insulted their mama and said some other shit that has made the owner of that haunted ass angry. Now you're scared, shivering, and lost, so *your* ass opens up. All of a sudden someone is digging in *your* ass. You're trying to get out of an ass while someone is all up in yours. So in a nutshell, before you go road rage and jump out of your car on someone, make sure your shit is in park.

Be aware of the type of ass you're getting into. Old people's asses are dangerous. Due to their years of experience, that can make it confusing. Trust me, you don't want a piece of an old person's ass. And last, never underestimate an ass. Like dogs' asses sense fear and shut down on you. A shut-down ass it not a place you wanna be.

Now, let's be clear, 'cause some of you look a bit confused. You don't want to wake up and physically be in someone's ass. When you go to the doctor and he puts two fingers in your ass, trust me, he doesn't want to be there. So if you're thinking to literally get into someone's ass, stop yourself. The only people that literally got in someone's ass were those fuckers in Lilliput. You know the story of that big ass giant Gulliver, right? He wandered into that town with those little people. Well, what you don't know is he fell asleep and those little muthafuckas tied him down, cut his throat, and dug a tunnel through his ass. They called it Gulliver's Tunnel.

They didn't put that shit in the book. To be honest, it was partly his fault—Lilliput was a bad neighborhood, and he was too nice of a guy to be walking in that part of town. You better believe a couple of those horny ass Lilliputians not only went into his ass, they fucked each other while in there. Eventually they developed his ass, built a strip club in there, food courts, all that shit. So always know who you're talking to, because if you're not careful, they'll get in your ass before you have a chance to get in theirs.

TOPSY-TURVY
(FLIP THAT SHIT)

𝕴 rarely take the advice of others. Oh, I'll take a lot of other stuff, like your lawn mower, your car, your eyeglasses, your cool ass top hat, your medication, your girl, my friend, my girl that I hit and quit and said you could have but now I'm gonna repo her back (that shit ain't just for cars), your virginity, your hospitality, your identity, your baby mama, your black nanny, your heart, and your soul—shit, I'll take your first love and your last slice of pizza. But one thing I usually never take from you is your advice.

All that said, here's some advice a friend of mine once gave me that I wholeheartedly agree with: There are times in life when you are going to have to take back a situation and turn the right side up to serve you. Sometimes you have to topsy-turvy the situation—basically flip that shit. Sometimes we get ourselves into bullshit.

For instance, I had a very important interview to go to, and my friend told me if that interview started to go sideways, that I needed to flip that shit. That is to say, take that damn interviewer and make him the damn interviewee. You topsy-turvy that goddamn interview! Here's what I mean: The interviewer says to you, "Tell me about your background." You say to them, "Actually, tell me about *your* background." See, now you're the one in control.

This is especially useful when you're courting a young woman and you gotta talk to her father for his approval. There's always a point in the relationship when you have to go to his house to let him decide if you're a good fit for his daughter. He'll ask you shit like, "Tell me about your last relationship, and do you have any children?" And instead of answering, you ask him the same shit, but you gotta be blunt. You ask him, "How many asses have you tapped in your lifetime? I'm thinking you're about sixty-five years old, let's say four to five taps a year, add that up—have you even counted?" At this point he's gonna smile, because he's remembering when he was your age, tapping ass. This moment will last only a second or two, because sooner or later he will get angry at you as he realizes you pulled the old switcheroo on him, which is what his generation called flipping that shit back in the day.

YOU CAN'T PAUSE TOAST

Once you put your bread in the toaster and press ON and it starts to toast, you can't press CANCEL, take it out, and then later on when you feel like it pop that bread back in to toast again. That shit just doesn't work. What I'm trying to say is that you can't go down certain roads unless you are ready to go all the way down them. You can't half break up with somebody, you gotta full-on break up and sever that tie.

You can't say "I love you" before you mean it, before it's time, because once you say it, you can't take it back and then try to say it again a month later.

The problem when someone says "I love you" is that the other person always feels fucking obligated to respond "I love you too." That fucking "too" in there. Like a goddamn parrot. You're either a grown ass man or a fucking parrot. Don't say it if you're not ready. If someone says "I love you" and you don't feel like saying it back, you just say, "Yeah, that's really cool." (Alternates are listed below.)

Remember: "Love" is a big ass motherfucking word. The "love" word will get your ass in trouble. Almost as much as the words "fuck it." See, unlike "Fuck!" which is just a reaction, FUCK IT are decision words. "Fuck" by itself is a beautiful thing, it's amazing. But then you add the "it," and you turn it into the opposite. Like you don't give a fuck about fucking!

Person A: Are we gonna fuck?
Person B: Nahhh, fuck it.

Look here, I know you're thinking you came to this chapter to read about toast and I gave you a bunch of love advice. And I can't lie, it might have sounded like I went off the rails a bit, but really, if you understand toast and toasters, then you know the connection.

You see, a relationship is like a toaster: Two pieces go in all fresh and naïve, but when they come out they are toast, perfect and ready for the world. Sometimes, though, that toaster is broken, it has a loose wire or a short or something and it becomes unpredictable; that's what it's like to be in a tumultuous relationship. Always being afraid that your partner is checking your phone, going through your emails—you know, tumultuous shit! Or crazy shit like super gluing your dick to your thigh while you sleep—well, shit, definitely while you're asleep, you let shit like that happen while you're awake, you've got bigger problems than I can fix. Or, I don't know, maybe you've got a broke ass dick that needed fixing. I don't know everybody's dick situation, and to be honest it ain't none of my business.

So anyway, one day you're using that tumultuous toaster, you set that damn timer and walk away and come back later to find that the toast popped out at the wrong time and it ain't toasted right. Now you're gonna want to push that bitch down 'cause you want that damn piece of toast, but you've got to think about it like this. If you left for work one day, kissed your lady on the lips, and went about your business, did all the day-to-day shit you always do, handled your grind all the while thinking about heading home to your lady, only to pull up in front of your house to find your personal shit spread every damn where, draws in the tree, neighbor's dog chewing on your slippers, and your Jordans hanging from a telephone wire, would you just gather all that shit up and take it in the house? Well, all your shit spread everywhere, that's the fucked up piece of toast.

Now I know people and I know tumultuous relationships, and that damn man staring at his shit everywhere, that dumb ass man's first thought is gonna be to run back in the house and try to save his relationship. What he is about to do is push that toast back down. And to be honest, if it's the first time he has paused that toast, he'll be able to get it back down, but trust me, that toast has already lost its essence. He'll apologize to his lady, promise to never do it again. Essentially he'll fiddle with that damn wire, hoping to fix the short. And she'll tell him she forgives him, but just know this: When a toaster has a short, you might as well just toss that shit out. See, 'cause even if she forgives, she doesn't forget, and you'll spend the rest of that relationship holding your breath, wondering when she's gonna bring that shit up again . . . that's a bad ass short.

See, you've pushed that toast back down, but you can't trust the timer; it's unpredictable. Either that shit's gonna come out too light or it's gonna burn the fucking house down. So now your lady starts hanging out late with her friends—she never did that before. Her new, unpredictable behavior causes you to do ridiculous things like calling her a million times when she hangs out. And that behavior causes her to not pick up and let your shit go to voicemail. Well, you're there all night staring at that toaster wondering what's going on, so you take a damn fork and jam it in there with it plugged in just to get that toast out! So with every desperate, embarrassing "Bitch, where you at?" call you make, you cheat as you jam that fork deeper and deeper into that damn toaster . . .

Then one day, like before, you kiss your lady and head off to work.

You do your day and handle your grind.

Five o'clock rolls around. And you head home . . .

Only to find your draws in a tree, the neighbor's dog chewing your slippers, and your Jordans hanging from that same damn telephone wire, only this time they're bleached and on fire. At that point, to let the world know that you've learned a valuable lesson I suggest you grab your phone, snap a nice picture of those damn majestic flaming Jordans—make sure it's not backlit and shit—and post it on Instagram with the caption #YouCantPauseToast.

CHAMPAGNE–FILLED
CROISSANTS

Now, I'm not trying to tell you to go out there, buy a bottle of
champagne, and try to pour it into a damn croissant. That shit is
messy—I know, I've tried it. Believe me, I've seen champagne poured into
some crazy places, shit I've been around. Look, a champagne-filled croissant is a fucking figure of speech! Just like when people say "I'm so hungry
I could eat a horse," they're not gonna eat no damn Sea Biscuit. First of all,
eating a horse is socially unacceptable, and second, that's too much damn
meat. When you hear champagne-filled croissants, it should immediately
take you to a place of decadence.

I will admit that the champagne-filled croissant sounds like some
French shit. I've been to Paris once, with Larry. I found it to be fucking
amazing! It didn't take long for me to learn a little French and start throwing some wee wee around. Now one thing about the French, they know
how to have a great time. They have a certain level of class and decadence
built into their culture.

Now, you don't have to be rich to understand decadence. We're talking
bougie shit, like a Rolls-Royce made out of sorbet, some caviar cookies,
or an eleven-piece pinstripe muthafuckin' suit. Just make sure you say it

right and fancy, and drop the "t." You can't say "hot dog" and be fancy, but saying "croissant" forces your decadent hand. Now, a champagne-filled croissant is a level of extreme decadence. If I'm living large and I'm doing something decadent, sitting on a heated toilet with my fuckin' feet up and eating seedless grapes while an Asian lady gives me a pedicure, and if someone calls my phone, I answer it and tell them what the fuck I'm doing. I tell them I'm having a champagne-filled croissant, and that fills their head with decadence. They close their fucking eyes and they envision the fucking croissant drenched in champagne—AWWW, nice. It's that unattainable kind of decadence, and everyone wants to do it, like opening a clam and finding an oyster inside. CF muthafuckin' C!

SOMEBODY ALWAYS GOTTA GET FUCKED UP, LARRY

𝕴'm not one to promote violence in any shape or form, but in the end when there's a conflict, there are only two scenarios, and in both somebody gets fucked up. It might be you, or it might be the other person. Just know that somebody's gonna get fucked up; there's no way around that shit. Even if it's got nothing to do with you and you're just watching shit go down, realize you are watching somebody get fucked up. It's the circle of life.

Remember when Larry wanted to look like a hero, so he asked me to snatch a purse from some lady and then he would swoop in and take it back from me? Well, I looked Larry in the eye and said:

You can't do that shit half-speed, you gotta get cued up to make it look real. I ain't gonna look like a goddamn bitch. Larry, you can't leave unscathed! Your glasses gotta be broke, your teeth gotta get chipped, gotta have one sneaker missing . . . bottom line, the more fucked up you look, the bigger the hero you'll be!

See, somebody's gotta get fucked up! If you're in a crazy brutal world, you can't do shit half-speed, you can't fake that I stole the purse and you wrestled that shit out of my hands. This ain't some even-Steven shit. I'm not gonna let some weak ass white man wrestle some damn Fendi, Channel, or Coach bag outta my damn hands! How the fuck does that sound?!? Plus, those purses are expensive—do you know much I could get for a name-brand bag like that at a pawn shop? Not that I know, or would ever engage in any sort of criminal venture of that nature.

Even in a relationship, someone is gonna get fucked up. Sometimes you are the fucker-upper, sometimes you are the one getting fucked.

I recommend y'all become bedroom fucker-uppers. It's a good reputation to have. You meet a lady, you don't leave that room all nice and clean, you fuck that room up. Empty that big ficus plant on the floor, knock shit over, break a mirror, a lamp, tear a hole in a pillow with your teeth—and make sure you pick the down pillow, not the synthetic shit (down pillows make a great fucking mess). If you really wanna strive, go for being the quicker fucker-upper: That means you're in and out of that muthafucka real quick, punching that clock in your mind. You hit it and quit it.

82 IS MY SHIT

My body works at a certain level. I'm optimized at 82. I can't live in a cold climate, my body don't adjust well. If I'm in someone's home and it's a white man's house—Larry's house is also set at fucking 70, his body works well in his temperature. I'm an 82 man myself. If your house is a 71, I'm getting goose bumps and shit. I'm in a bad mood. Nothing more punk ass than a fucking dude with chill bumps on his arms. How many times have I seen them stupid ass chill bumps on their stupid ass arms, I look at this muthafucka with disgust. You're talking to me about some shit and you got chill bumps? That's some disgusting shit. I don't want to talk to you no more. 'Cause you got chill bumps. How can we talk about football with those chill bumps? What else can you talk about? Maybe the time your grandmother didn't buy you that fucking doll when you were a kid?? When I go to someone's house, they always have that shit set at 69. They walk around in fucking pajamas with that stupid hat and that stupid ass pajama top. Then you make sense, 'cause a nightcap is when you bring a lady, you get tipsy, and then you get fucking. How did they relate a nightcap to a fucking hat that you wear when you're sleeping by yourself?

I sleep naked. I just get in bed with my clothes on. I take them off under the covers. But if some bullshit is going down, or some crazy noises, I'll pull my boxer briefs back on. You can't fight a monster with your fucking Johnson dangling and shit. The monsters always go for the Johnson first—the first thing they're gonna grab is your junk, and then swing you around the room by your junk. That happened to me a bunch of fucking times. Like you're a fucking yo-yo.

Believe me, I have fought people butt ass naked, and it's not cool. Especially if they're all in clothes and weaponized. That shit ain't cool. If you ever feel threatened in someone's house, if I'm in your house or spending the night, I'm wearing my fucking underwear and shoes. Tie 'em real tight. You can't fight barefoot. It's not easy, it only works if they are fucking barefoot too. But if not, that's not a fair fight.

That's how I doozit.

END AND
ENDINGS

STEP OUT THAT ASS

Well, that's it! Everything that begins has to end, so this is the end of the book. Having to end this shit got me thinking about endings. When you say the word "ending" out loud, it sounds final. I mean, you hear on the news about a muthafucka driving at 100 MPH who hit a wall and met his end—now, that's final. And to be honest, in that case, he did meet his end. When you think about his ass, it probably did slam into his head; that is the definition of a person meeting his damn end. But that is an example of a final end. To be honest, most ends lead to a beginning, if you let them. Take me, for instance. One day I got a call from my sister, inviting me to come live with her at some rich ass Jewish man's place. Cut to years later, that rich Jewish man is even richer, he and my sister have broken up, she, my auntie, and the kids are gone, I'm living with *him* and he's *my* rich ass Jewish friend. Actually, he became more than a friend: that man is family. Now I know you might think that I'm taking advantage of him, Larry might even think that sometimes, but every time he tries to bring up some bullshit like that, I remind him that we have an even steven relationship, tit for tat if you will. I give that man just as much as he gives me. We have shared a lot of shit. I taught him many things, like how to lamp or do the dizzle, and he got me eating shit like borscht, gefilte fish, and matzo ball soup. That's some of the tastiest, nastiest shit I've ever eaten! I have had a lot of good times with that man and plan to have a lot more, but eventually this shit will have to end. Sometimes I get sad looking at him puttering around his house, doing things like looking for his glasses while they are sitting on top of his head, and I wonder to myself what shit he's gonna leave me in his will. He's got a lot of shit: white shit, like golf clubs, vases, deck shoes, et cetera.

Look, life is like a long climb up a mountain. When it starts off, it's not too scary, but eventually, the higher you go, the more dangerous it gets. As you climb, sometimes the moves are easy: You pick the right friend or the right job or the right partner . . . But sometimes the moves get tricky: You have bills, you get divorced, you get sick, things like that. Every now and then, though, you find a little ledge: tiny but kind of safe—not safe enough to live on, but safe enough to stay awhile, get your shit together, drink a little water, and plan your next move. I've been sitting on one of those ledges for a while now, and soon it will be time to leave, but I'll never forget this ledge. It means everything for me to have it. As you know by now, the ledge I refer to is a metaphor—unless of course you are one of those crazy ass muthafuckas who actually climb mountains, in which case I have to ask you, "Why the fuck do you climb mountains? *You're* probably one of those people who are able to parasail on a Tuesday workday. Must be fuckin' nice."

Anyway, back to the rest of you: In the metaphor I just created, that little ledge can represent a lot of things: a rehab center, going back to school, finding a briefcase full of clean, unmarked bills, et cetera. In my case, though, that ledge was a white man with a bald head, long balls, and a huge heart. And one day, there will come an end to this chapter in my life, and I will have to move on and let all this fancy shit go.

And on that day, I will look that lanky white man in the eyes, fist bump his lanky white hand, thank him for everything, and say, "I left you some Chinese food up in my room on that goddamn twin bed. LD, you take care. I'm out."